IT'S NEVER TOO LATE TO FIND YOUR CROWN

JeanAnne Roberts

It's Never Too Late to Find Your Crown
Trilogy Christian Publishers

A Wholly Owned Subsidiary of Trinity Broadcasting Network

2442 Michelle Drive, Tustin, CA 92780

Copyright © 2024 by JeanAnne Roberts

Scripture quotations marked ESV are taken from the ESV® Bible (The Holy Bible, English Standard Version®), copyright © 2001 by Crossway Bibles, a publishing ministry of Good News Publishers. Used by permission. All rights reserved.

Scripture quotations marked GW are taken from GOD'S WORD®, © 1995 God's Word to the Nations. Used by permission of God's Word Mission Society.

Scripture quotations marked NASB are taken from the New American Standard Bible® (NASB), Copyright © 1960, 1962, 1963, 1968, 1971, 1972, 1973, 1975, 1977, 1995 by The Lockman Foundation. Used by permission. www.Lockman.org.

Scripture quotations marked ERV are taken from the Holy Bible: Easy-to-Read Version (ERV), International Edition© 2013, 2016 by Bible League International and used by permission.

Scripture quotations marked NIV are taken from the Holy Bible, New International Version®, NIV®. Copyright © 1973, 1978, 1984, 2011 by Biblica, Inc.™ Used by permission of Zondervan. All rights reserved worldwide. www.zondervan.com. The "NIV" and "New International Version" are trademarks registered in the United States Patent and Trademark Office by Biblica, Inc.™

Scripture quotations marked NLT are taken from the Holy Bible, New Living Translation, copyright © 1996, 2004, 2015 by Tyndale House Foundation. Used by permission of Tyndale House Publishers, Inc., Carol Stream, Illinois 60188. All rights reserved.

Scripture quotations marked NKJV are taken from the New King James Version®. Copyright © 1982 by Thomas Nelson. Used by permission. All rights reserved.

Scripture quotations marked KJV are taken from the King James Version of the Bible. Public domain.

All rights reserved, including the right to reproduce this book or portions thereof in any form whatsoever.

For information, address Trilogy Christian Publishing

Rights Department, 2442 Michelle Drive, Tustin, CA 92780.

Trilogy Christian Publishing/ TBN and colophon are trademarks of Trinity Broadcasting Network.

For information about special discounts for bulk purchases, please contact Trilogy Christian Publishing.

Trilogy Disclaimer: The views and content expressed in this book are those of the author and may not necessarily reflect the views and doctrine of Trilogy Christian Publishing or the Trinity Broadcasting Network.

10 9 8 7 6 5 4 3 2 1

Library of Congress Cataloging-in-Publication Data is available.

ISBN: 979-8-89333-301-5

ISBN: 979-8-89333-302-2

Forever Grateful

I would like to thank first and foremost,
my God through which all blessings flow.

I would like to thank my beloved husband who made it possible for me to compete for "Mrs. DC America 2020." Your love and devotion to me and our family is a real-life fairytale.

Thank you to my mom who expected nothing
less than greatness from all her children.

Thank you to my sister, Wendy Griffith, who became a co-host with Pat Robertson on the 700 Club starting her career working as an assistant at a local tv station in Yuma, Arizona. She showed me "with persistence, passion, and honoring God" it can be done.

Thank you to my brothers Pete and Truman Griffith
and their lovely brides who sponsored me to represent
DC on the Mrs. America Stage.

Thank you to Lisa Gooslin for sponsoring my Mrs. America Swarovski High Heel Shoes in honor of her beloved mother who was a Girl Scout leader.

Thank you to Marta Bota who coached me with "Passion for Pageantry," being an integral part to win the crown.

Thank you to Kathy Keller "Forever Friend" and Dr. Bunin "Family Dentist" for believing in me and sponsoring my fee to compete for the title of Mrs. DC America 2020.

I would like to thank my "Super Model Bestie" Debra Ovall who called me as soon as I won the crown and said it inspired her. That inspired me.

Thank you to Cemo Basen, the next "Johnny Depp," for being my social media manager.

Thank you to Cheryl Felicia Rhoads (LA Acting Coach) and owner of Cheryl Felicia Rhoads Northern Virginia Acting School who prepared me for the crown and beyond and Maryland Acting Coach Katie Killacky, owner of Capital Coaching.

Thank you to Kristina Christopher, The PR Team, true talent.

Thank you to Emerly Drye, "Beauty Specialist & Superwoman," who was the Makeup/Hair team for Randhawa Brands NYFW September 2023 for sixty models.

Thank you to (actress/model) Bellina Lambdin who believed my story was newsworthy and got it published in "Viva Tyson's Magazine."

Thank you to Model/Actor Becky Freemont who was a sponsor for both productions, "Mr. DC and Singles in the City – DC."

Thank you to Josephine Armar (actress /model) and Lilia Damien (English teacher /runway model) for proofreading my first draft.

Thank you to all the amazing women I met on the Mrs. America stage and specifically Lakeisha Lemons, Miss DC for America 2020, true beauty, and queen.

Thank you, Kim Ward, my best friend from my college days for coming alongside me and walking the New York runway. Dreams come true!

Thank you to "blonde beauty" Elizabeth Krueger, who I met on vacation in the Atlantis, Bahamas. Her daughters Ava and Grace are two of the top Irish Dancers in the world. She knows competition and she encouraged me and believed I could capture the crown.

Thank you to Afsheen Ather/ Nova Derm Institute, sponsored skincare specialist/ antiaging expert during my reign and beyond.

Thank you to Kim Dixon "Physical Therapist" for keeping me for keeping me supermodel ready!

Thank you, "Diamond Lake Jewelry," for featuring me as a model for your luxury brand.

Thank you to Jenny Moon/Owner of Magic Skin Clinic for showing me that Korean facials turn back time!

Thank you Coressa Williams owner of "Princess for a Day" and Ozzy Ramos founder of "American Veterans Ball" for the honor of being ambassadors for your exclusive brands.

Thank you to so many designers including Troy Anthony for choosing me to be a spokesmodel for his upscale brand, Mariam Heydari for hiring me to showcase her show stopping pieces and Star Lashelle for selecting me to walk for her resort brand.

Thank you, "Crown Sponsors," who are the finest bridal /fashion makeup artists in the DMV and beyond, Mervat Haddad, Nour Silver and Alina Karaman.

Thank you to Michelle Blake "The Body" for being my personal trainer and inspirational coach.

Thank you to husband /wife team, Murat and Gulchin, owners of SoChicSalonVA for being amazing stylists and color specialists.

Thank you to extraordinary fashion/wedding/headshots DMV Photographers: Focus Fine Photography Tanira Dove Photography, Alimond Studio, Anthony Conoway "Classic Portraits," Stephan George, John Wardell, Renee Wilhite, Sarosh Mir, Sid Portrait, and Roy Cox "Official Pageant Photographer for 2020."

Thank you to Rodney Branche "Copa Style Magazine' who keeps DC informed on the newest beauty and fashion trends for each season.

Thank you to Amna Inam for understanding the power of the crown and choosing me to be the Show Opener & Choreographer for Randhawa Brands NYFW February 2023 /September and February 2024.

Thank you to Beth Miller who helped coach me with my most important answer for "Why I should be chosen as Mrs. DC America 2020." It truly is a higher calling.

Thank you to my beloved Girl Scouts and parents.

Thank you to Hotel Edison Times Square NYC for treating me like a Royalty.

Thank you to my manager, Tony Marinozzi "LA Screen Writer" for inspiring me to write my story.

Thank you to God for putting an anointed crown on my head to inspire millions that it is not too late.

Standing Ovation

It's Never Too Late to Find Your Crown, is a masterfully heartwarming tale of a woman's journey through life, overcoming challenges and beating the odds, to finally finding her "Crown." Receiving the coveted title of "Mrs. District of Columbia (DC)" in 2020, during the height of a world-wide pandemic and competing against women much younger, JeanAnne Roberts shows that with perseverance, grit, and a foundation of faith, our aspirations are indeed reachable. This book is a fantastic read, especially for those who question the strength of their dreams; it will motivate and inspire you to believe and fight for them!

Jeff Ovall

Author of *The Man Who Saved Christmas*
and *Chronicles of the Hedge*

JeanAnne Roberts offers the reader fifty-five short chapters that are packed with captivating stories, humor, great advice, and faith.

After reading this book, you will realize that's it's never too late to achieve your dreams, rejection is an opportunity for improvement, determination and Perseverance can move mountains.

- Michelle Blake, M.S., Blake LLC, Personal Trainer, and Motivational Coach

Table of Contents

Prelude – Almost Heaven — 15
1. Chapter: Buried Dreams — 17
2. Chapter: Mrs. DC America 2020 — 21
3. Chapter: Virtual Pageant — 23
4. Chapter: The Competition & The Winning Answer — 27
5. Chapter: Mrs. Georgetown America 2020 — 31
6. Chapter: The Royal Crown — 35
7. Chapter: The Picture — 39
8. Chapter: The Road to the Crown — 41
9. Chapter: Bestower of Crowns — 45
10. Chapter: Miss Mingo County — 49
11. Chapter: Junior Miss Pageant — 51
12. Chapter: College Years — 53
13. Chapter: A Man's World — 55
14. Chapter: Country Roads — 59
15. Chapter: Graduate School & The Dangerous Liaisons — 61
16. Chapter: A Child is Born — 65
17. Chapter: New York State of Mind — 69
18. Chapter: The Gift — 71
19. Chapter: Everything that Glitter's isn't Gold — 73
20. Chapter: The Greatest Love — 77
21. Chapter: The Cross and the Crown — 81
22. Chapter: My Daughter — 83
23. Chapter: The Sheriff — 87
24. Chapter: Love from Pakistan — 91
25. Chapter: The Four-Legged Prince — 95
26. Chapter: Becoming Queen — 97
27. Chapter: The Cherry Blossom Dress — 101
28. Chapter: New Horizons — 105

29.	Chapter: Bath Robes to Royal Robes	109
30.	Chapter: Be Okay With You	113
31.	Chapter: The Hidden Cost	117
32.	Chapter: The History of Beauty Pageants	119
33.	Chapter: Creating Mr. DC	121
34.	Chapter: Au Natural	125
35.	Chapter: Heartbreak in Pittsburgh	129
36.	Chapter: My Pageant Playbook	133
37.	Chapter: Competing for Mrs. America	135
38.	Chapter: Helping Others	141
39.	Chapter: The Judge	145
40.	Chapter: Singles in the City – DC	147
41.	Chapter: Walk by Faith	151
42.	Chapter: Still Standing	155
43.	Chapter: The Dentist and the Crown	159
44.	Chapter: The Competitors	161
45.	Chapter: Family Ties	163
46.	Chapter: Standing on Holy Ground	165
47.	Chapter: A Blink of an Eye	167
48.	Chapter: Fashion is not for the Faint of Heart	169
49.	Chapter: Beauty Tips from the Queen	171
50.	Chapter: New York Fashion Week 2023	175
51.	Chapter: The Housewife	179
52.	Chapter: It's not Impossible	183
53.	Chapter: Ray of Light	185
54.	Chapter: No Media Requests	187
55.	Chapter: The Team	189

Almost Heaven

"Honour your father and thy mother, that thy days may be long upon the land which the Lord thy God giveth thee " Exodus 20:12 (KJV).

My mom was a young mom in her early twenties. She had short naturally curly hair, the perfect figure, and a beautiful face. She looked like my starlets from that era. She also had three little girls. When my baby sister, Nancy, was one, I was five, and my sister Wendy was six. My dad was a traveling salesman, so my mom took care of us alone. My mom worked tirelessly to take care of us from washing clothes, making breakfast before school, preparing a warm meal every night and endless cleaning of dirty dishes which made my mom's hands raw. From a child's mind, I did not realize that my mom had the world on her shoulders.

When I was in kindergarten, I remember putting my head on the desk and crying. My teacher would ask me why I was sad. Being too embarrassed to tell her, I just needed a hug from my mom.

My father worked for Baxter Pharmaceuticals. He was tall, dark, and handsome, and had a smile that would light up the room. I remember him walking in the door with the familiar scent of Old Spice. We would line up and wait for him to give us piggyback rides. The amazing thing about this scent is the first time I met my husband; he smelled like my dad. I asked him what he was wearing, and it was the same cologne. It brought back memories of days gone by and happy times spent with my young father.

My story begins in "Almost Heaven West Virginia" with its majestic mountains, rolling hills and valleys, and fresh mountain air. This is where I was born, where my family originated and where I will always feel home. I am a direct descendant of the Hatfield's and McCoy's. My great great great Uncle Devil Anse was the leader of the Hatfield Clan. This was considered one of the most infamous feuds in American History. This feud originally started over a pig. It then turned into a land dispute which led to a battle between two families lasting for more than a hundred years.

I did not realize as a child that in my future I would also fight many battles. Even through endless failure, I would get back up with perseverance and determination like my ancestors. I would find God, true love, success and in the end realize "It is never too late to find your Crown."

Chapter 1

Buried Dreams

"Lift up your heads, O you gates; be lifted up, you ancient door, that the King of glory shall come in"

Psalms 24:7 (NKJV)

When I decided to run for Mrs. DC America in 2020, the memory of losing the crown at the Junior Miss Pageant in Mingo County, West Virginia some thirty-six years earlier came flooding back. I had given it my all and didn't even place in the top three. I was devastated, remembering the disappointment I felt and how I feared I had let everyone down, especially my mom. I asked myself what I could have done differently but didn't have a clue. At just eighteen years old, I felt like a failure and certainly believed that my pageant days were over. But God wasn't done writing my story. Now, at the age of fifty-five, I was about to learn that failure is not final and that it's never too late to find your crown.

After a decade long career as an international flight attendant and later a stay-at-home mom with two teenagers, the time felt right. I had sat in a corner too long watching everyone else succeed. My (Irish Twin) sister was a famous news anchor and reporter, my younger sister was one of the glamorous (Housewives of Coraopolis), and both of my brothers were successful attorneys. God was unearthing a dream buried deep in my heart that was still very much alive and at fifty-five years old, I was ready to take on the biggest challenge of my life and compete with women, some decades younger than me, for the title of Mrs. DC America. But this time, I would prepare like Esther and train like Rocky. I had the sense that God wanted to give me more than a crown and a title. This was about fulfilling my destiny.

This pageant was about beauty and brains, much like the Junior Miss Pageant from years ago. I had to choose a platform and had two months to prepare. I couldn't help wondering if it was too late. I believe this feeling of being old had haunted me since my college years. In that era, women still met their husbands in high school or at college, getting married in their early twenties. There were still not a lot of career opportunities for women at that time. And I was a hopeless romantic, just like Renee Zellweger in Bridget Jones Diary, looking for the fairytale. But after my first love had broken up with me, I felt unloved and defeated. I knew I had to get back up and find my crown again.

Still single at the age of thirty-five, I went to a casting call for several New York Modeling Agencies. They told me they loved my look, but said I was too old to be a model. Having this lifelong dream, I felt like Anne Hathaway in the classic movie The Devil Wears Prada which ignited an entire generation of passion for fashion.

That same year, I broke up with my tennis pro fiancé and the man I'd been dating for two years. I will not deny he was charming, but I knew in my heart he wasn't the one. Everyone told me, you'll never find another eligible man at your age. But two years later, I met my husband to be at the age of thirty-eight and we have been happily married ever since.

Fortunately, I never took my coworkers and friends well-meaning words of advice. I knew that with God, all things are possible and that I had a choice to give up or give it all I have. I chose the latter.

My message to you is, You're not too old! It's not too late! And perhaps, just like He did for me, God is setting you up for an epic comeback story! God wants to give you the desires of your heart and rekindle buried dreams – He never forgets, even when we do. What dream does God need to awaken in your heart? Maybe it's time to let Him do it.

I pray my story will encourage you to go for all that God has for you, because just like Rocky and Esther, you can win the title and receive the crown.

Chapter 2

Mrs. DC America 2020

> *"You will also be a crown of beauty in the hand of the Lord.*
> *And a royal diadem in the hand of your God"*
>
> **Isaiah 62:3 (NKJV)**

What gave me the courage to step on that stage? I remember walking on the beach and crying endless tears over years of rejection from men. Like I said before, I wanted to find the fairytale, true love and marriage. Why was it so easy for other twenty and thirty somethings to find true love? Some of my coworkers in the airline industry had already been married twice. Thirty-five and still single, I was told by society that I was too old to get married, I was too old to have children and I was too old to pursue a modeling career. This is what fueled my fire and led me to this moment. At the age of fifty-five, I was now happily married and wanted to inspire millions to not give up because it is never too late to find love, get married, have children, pursue your dreams, and find your crown.

God wanted me to first and foremost be an example for my beloved daughter, KellyAnne, and encourage all the women who have been beaten down throughout life that you are not too old, and it is not too late. There is a movie called *Under the Tuscan Sun*. At the end of the movie, Diane Lane says a monumental phrase, "Unthinkably good things can happen, even late in the game."

I did not have the beauty of my youth. At the age of fifty-five, I was told I had a different beauty. I had womanly curves. I have given birth twice, once a natural birth and the second a c-section. My once perfectly flat stomach was not perfectly flat anymore. I had scars to show the sacrifice of giving birth and bringing life into this world.

I had been married for almost fifteen years when I won the crown. Marriage is a divine law created by God between man and woman. Our culture glamorizes divorce, cheating, and the single life. I wanted to show women and men that marriage is beautiful. The Bible states that the marriage bed between a couple is the most intense emotion you will ever experience in this lifetime. And finally, I wanted to encourage marriage and family because it creates a strong community and world. In Proverbs 12:4, it states, an excellent wife is the crown of her husband.

The crown, to me, also represents Christ. We must share the message of Christianity and glorify God's name on this earth. My platform was mentoring young girls. We must prepare our next generation of leaders by teaching them Godly principles and by wearing the crown, it has given me a voice to reach young people and beyond. William Shakespeare said, "Heavy is the head that wears the crown."

Chapter 3

Virtual Pageant

"For nothing will be impossible with God"

Luke 1:37 (ESV)

It was 2020 and everything was shut down. But the Mrs. DC America Pageant must go on because this was a yearly competition and the preliminary to Mrs. America.

As a contestant, I was judged on interview, bathing suit, walk and gown.

The pageant was to be held at the historic Kennedy Center. John F. Kennedy envisioned this to provide a beautiful building for performing arts for events such as ballets, musicals, operas etc. After his assassination, they committed this building to him. The opening night of this significant landmark was a Catholic Mass service in honor of his life.

Getting ready for this moment, I was thinking back on all the significant moments that had prepared me for this stage. Even though there were so many times throughout my life when I thought God had truly forgotten me, he was behind the scenes creating a beautiful symphony. The final decision for the pageant was that all contestants would compete virtually due to the pandemic. My husband set up the basement like a magnificent stage with the camera on a tripod and lights everywhere.

The first segment was the interview. This was held at 11 a.m. My hair was styled by Merry Valdez owner of Celebrities Salon and Spa. Names are powerful and this salon was befitting of noble beginnings. The makeup artist was Marta Bota, over the age of fifty, less makeup makes you look more youthful, and that was her specialty.

There were six star studded judges on the panel to select the queen. These included Mrs. DC America 2018 Leiah Rocheleau, Princess Grace Kelly look alike, Stacey Adams, owner of Fitness Together in Georgetown who resembled American actress Julia Roberts, Candiace Dillard Bassett reality star featured on the *Real Housewives of Potomac* reminiscent of the iconic Vanessa Williams, Jay Rocheleau a doppelganger for Ryan Reynolds who was a national motivational speaker, and a local cosmetic dentist with the perfect smile.

Each judge asked me a different question. After hundreds of hours of preparation, I was happy to answer and felt confident that I did my absolute best and spoke from my heart. The first question was to name three qualities to describe yourself. My first quality was, I am committed. I have been married to my husband for over fourteen years. As a Mrs. contestant, I understand true commitment and believe I can bring this commitment to the Mrs. America Pageant System. Service is my second quality. As a flight attendant, I served customers domestic and international for over a decade. The third quality is I am a leader. I was appointed to oversee the local Girl Scout troop during my reign. My platform was mentoring young girls to become future leaders. Commitment, service, and leadership are three qualities I hold close to my heart.

After the interview segment, we had a scheduled time to model our bathing suits. In this system, no bikinis, we were required to wear a one-piece suit. When I saw the blue bathing suit on Amazon, I knew this was the winning look. This bathing suit was identical to the one-piece bathing suit with ruffles I had worn on stage at the age of seventeen for Miss Magnolia Fair. I wonder if this was a coincidence, or a God ordained moment.

The next section was evening gown. Searching the internet, I found the most beautiful white pageant gown embellished with Swarovski crystals at an online store called Peaches based in Chicago. All the stores were closed because of Covid. White was the winning color in pageantry. As I walked to the camera to show off this beautiful gown, memories of the Junior Miss Pageant came flooding back. So many tears had fallen from my cheeks but this time, I was smiling.

Then it was time for the final question. When they asked me, "Why I believed I should be chosen to be the next Mrs. DC America 2020?" I was so nervous that I made my husband hide behind a partition in the basement. I was more intimidated by my husband than the judges. He was a director of finance for millions of dollars for a startup company called Spark Fund. He was a realist, and I was a dreamer.

When they announced the 1st runner up, I waited with childhood innocence. Even though I had experienced so much heartache throughout my life, I still had hope to win the crown. After they called the first runner up, I knew it was possible. Before they announced the winner, God spoke to me and said, "YOU ARE ANNOINTED AND APPOINTED." Then the announcer called my name and my life changed instantly. My husband jumped up from behind the partition with a radiant smile, my kids ran downstairs and hugged me. In that moment, I realized I had achieved the impossible. A small-town girl originally from the mountains of West Virginia had won the crown of Mrs. DC America against woman thirty years younger and now would be going to compete for the coveted title of Mrs. America at the age of fifty-five.

Chapter 4

The Competition & The Winning Answer

"Do you know that in a race all the runners run, but only one receives the prize? So run that you may obtain it"

1 Corinthians 9:24 (ESV)

This pageant was the Mrs. DC America Pageant, and the winner would compete for Mrs. America. This iconic pageant system is the second oldest pageant system after Miss America in the country. It has been around for forty-six years. This pageant was created to honor married women who are devoted to their family, the community, and their profession.

Thinking back to my childhood, when I was a little girl, my mom, dad, and sisters would sit in the family room watching all the beautiful women compete from each State for the coveted crown.

Entering this competition, I realized the magnitude of this event and the impact of the crown.

For this competition, we were competing at the state level, so the competition was fierce! This was not the majestic mountains of West Virginia anymore, I was competing for the title of D.C., the most powerful stage in the world.

I had five competitors seeking the title and the crown; the first young lady competing was a beautiful twenty-five-year-old newlywed, the second powerful lady was a Navy captain, the third compassionate lady was a nurse, the fourth glamorous lady was an international model and the fifth intelligent lady competing for the crown was an attorney at law.

My mom had always encouraged my dad to be an attorney. He took the LSAT and was accepted to law school but because he had a young family, he could not pursue that goal. He was already a successful salesman and continued in that profession for his entire career. My mom encouraged all my siblings to become lawyers. It was a very prestigious and lucrative career. I took a prep course for the LSAT but to me, it was like a foreign language. I could not understand it. I never succeeded in the business world. I loved fashion, traveling, and helping others.

All the ladies competing for the crown were young, accomplished and in the work force. I had been a stay-at-home mom for the last twelve years. My daughter was eighteen months younger than my son. They were now eleven and thirteen. Thinking back to the hospital room, the minute they placed my son in my arms, I chose the career of homemaker. I had been working since my teenage years. My first job was working at a Dairy Queen. A very befitting name for a future queen. After twenty plus years in the work force, I was happy to be hired for the position of "mom."

Now, after an era, I was ready to get back in the ring! This was more than a competition for me, I wanted to make my mom proud. I remembered that moment thirty-six years ago like it had happened yesterday. I had to rewrite the story but this time it would be on a bigger stage and for a higher calling. I also wanted to show my daughter and inspire women of all ages that you can be beautiful, accomplished and make a difference.

As I stepped on stage to answer the final question, I thought of all the women that had taken a risk, had influence and even lost their lives standing up for what they believed in. Then the host asked me "Why do you believe you should be chosen as the next Mrs. DC America 2020?" I have practiced this answer hundreds of times with my coach, my daughter, my son, my husband, and my dearest friends. I searched my heart and prayed over and over for the winning answer. At that moment, God revealed the answer to this question.

My answer to the host, the judges, my parents, and the entire world was "I have been waiting for this moment for thirty-six years. And after all this time and all my life experiences, I believe now that I am truly worthy to wear this crown. And with this crown, I will mentor young girls to be future leaders through the Girl Scouts of the United States of America, I will help the needs of the community and I will show the world that this pageant system is not just a beauty pageant, it is a higher calling."

Chapter 5

Mrs. Georgetown America 2020

"I am the vine; you are the branches. If a man remains in me and I in him, he will bear much fruit; apart from me you can do nothing"

John 15:5 (ERV)

After paying the registration fee, I was appointed Mrs. Georgetown America 2020. This was a local title. Five other women were also designated local crowns. We would be competing against each other for the state title of Mrs. DC America in the coming months.

My first encounter with Georgetown was at the age of eighteen. My sister Wendy and I had been invited to stay with a great aunt during Christmas break. Meeting her for the first time, she had a regal presence with striking red hair, reminiscent of my high school boyfriend's. She had a flare for fashion and lived in an exclusive community in Bethesda, Maryland. We both got holiday jobs in Georgetown, working in an upscale boutique. I do not remember a lot of details, but I remember meeting people from all over the world. The city was an exciting place and quite different from the rural mountains of West Virginia.

Fast forward many years, I always felt a special connection to Georgetown. I loved this charming historic destination. One of the oldest taverns in Georgetown, locally owned for four generations, Martin's Tavern, is where John F. Kennedy proposed to Jaclyn Bouvier. Sequoia DC is another lovely restaurant with its dramatic river views and swanky design having the most spacious terrace on the waterfront overlooking luxury yachts and the historic Kennedy Center. This is where I had my bachelorette party fifteen years before. Annie Chien, General Manager of Sequoia DC, approved the request and was the most generous sponsor for both of my recent productions, Mr. DC, and Singles in the City - DC. This area also has an array of boutiques, bars, and bakeries. If you are a cupcake lover, Georgetown Cupcakes is my favorite.

When I first moved to DC at the age of twenty-nine, my sister and I lived in Rosslyn, Virginia, this was within walking distance of Georgetown. To get to this iconic location, we would walk across the Key Bridge. My sister Wendy had recently moved to DC where she was hired as a reporter for CBN. I had been living in Pittsburg previously as a flight attendant with my other flight attendant sister Nancy. Unfortunately, I had another terrible heartbreak and decided to move to DC and start a new beginning. I love the song by Garth Brooks, "Thank God for Unanswered Prayers" because even when we pray for a specific love, some of God's greatest gifts are unanswered prayers!

Now that I had the title of Mrs. Georgetown, I began to research this waterfront community and found out something astonishing. The famous singer, John Denver had helped write the song "Take me Home, Country Roads" at a bar called the "Cellar Door" in Georgetown. It all began when a songwriter wanted him to review the lyrics. He had recently seen a postcard of West Virginia and fallen in love with its beauty. The song was supposed to be about Maryland, but John Denver got permission to change it to West Virginia. He stood up on stage that evening and sang that song to the audience. The crowd gave him a standing ovation and that was his first number one hit! I knew I had a connection to Georgetown. Those country roads were not far from home.

Chapter 6

The Royal Crown

"Behold, I come quickly; hold that fast which thou hast, that no man take thy crown"

Revelations 3:11 (KJV)

After winning the crown, I went to New York to get pictures with my amazing New York Photography Team, David, and Lena Kaptein. My state director had booked photos with a local photographer, but it would be several months before they could take the official picture for Mrs. DC America 2020.

As the new queen, I needed a powerful picture to represent the District of Columbia for the Mrs. America Stage.

In New York, the makeup artist, Lena Kaptein, used her favorite makeup brand called Bravon. While taking pictures, they also did a video. In the video she mentioned I was wearing Bravon Makeup and she posted this on an Instagram Story.

When I returned home from the photoshoot, I was so excited because these pictures represented the crown, and I was ready to begin my reign.

I then received a call from the publicist. This lady was a former pageant queen who had competed for Miss Pennsylvania America "the same system" three times and won the coveted crown. Her duties were being an assistant to my DC State Director and the public relations person for my reign.

When I answered the phone, she said that I had violated the contract and would have to sign for my first violation. After this, I would have two more chances before they would take my crown. This violation policy was not in the contract. What had I done? I had worked a lifetime to prepare and win this crown and now this sly assistant was telling me they could take it from me. I felt like Vanessa Williams at that moment. But my crime was wearing someone else's makeup.

My director had just started selling her own line of lashes and eyeshadow. I was happy to promote her and felt very committed to the Mrs. DC America Brand. I was then told I had promoted another makeup line and that was against the contract.

I am an honest person and was broken-hearted that anyone would accuse me of doing this on purpose. I am a Christian and do my best to uphold Godly principles. At that moment I knew I had to fight to keep my crown.

I was not just a country girl from the mountains of West Virginia anymore. And I had a team of lawyers ready to defend my honor. Both of my brothers were ready to defend me. My youngest brother, Truman, is a personal injury lawyer, my older brother Pete is a public defender/judge, and my Uncle Truman was a prestigious state senator and the owner of Chafin Law Firm. My Uncle Truman's first case was a young man who lost his arm in a mining accident. He did not have money to pay for representation, my uncle was so moved, he represented him and made millions on his first case. Sometimes, money isn't everything. God saw and blessed my uncle for having a heart like David.

My first cousins Kurt, Lori, and Moses are also legal counselors, and the list goes on.

Immediately, I contacted both of my brothers and sent them the contract. They read it and said the contract was very vague. They told me to sign the first violation and let my state director and her assistant know if they had any other problems to contact my attorneys.

I am happy to say I did not have any other violations; I would wear the crown with honor.

Chapter 7

The Picture

"Commit your work to the Lord and your plans will be established"

Proverbs 16:3 (ESV)

After getting my modeling pictures with David and Lena, I was ready to book some modeling jobs. I went back to the DMV and immediately saw a job on a freelance site called DragonukConnects. The advertisement said they were looking for models for a fashion segment on Fox 5. I was excited to submit my New York headshot. After submitting, I was contacted the next day and was told I had been selected to be a model for the segment. The dress code for the models was holiday attire to promote fashion for the Christmas and Holiday Season. I love fancy dresses and had the perfect one! My favorite dress in my closet was a rose gold sequin mini dress from Bebe.

The fashion segment was scheduled for the next week, so I anxiously awaited this moment. After quitting my job at Swarovski, I had started my pursuit of my modeling dream, but at the age of fifty-four, I had not had any luck. I spent over four thousand dollars to find the right photographer. It seemed like a lifetime since my last job opportunity. My last was fourteen years before and I had been chosen to try out for the face of Avon. It was disappointing not to be chosen for this prestigious brand, but I had other exciting moments ahead. At the age of forty, I got engaged, married, and pregnant. I had forgotten all about my modeling dreams.

My dream had been reawakened, I had booked the job and would be on live TV. As soon as I walked into the studio, I was greeted by a beautiful lady wearing a red top and a black princess skirt. She looked at me and said I was going to be the next Mrs. DC America 2020. I was so confused and surprised by this response. She introduced herself as the director for Mrs. DC America. I then responded by saying I thought I might be too old to compete for a pageant, but she said, "You are a timeless beauty." I realized at that moment that God had seen that buried dream in my heart from many years ago.

This reminds me of a true story of a famous portrait in the Louvre. This painting shows the devil and a man playing chess, named *Checkmate*. The artist makes it appear as if the devil has won the chess game. The devil is smiling, and the man is looking down in desperation.

A group of athletes were on a guided tour. One of the men in the group was a world champion chess player. The group glanced at the painting and went to the next one, but the world champion chess player stood staring at the board. What he realized was astounding! He saw that "the king had one more move." This is how life can be.

When I lost the Junior Miss Pageant at the age of eighteen, I never thought I would have another opportunity to compete in another state competition. Then thirty-six years later, the opportunity presented itself. I thought I had been defeated but the good news is, just like in the game of chess, "the king had one more move." In my case, the Queen!!

Chapter 8

The Road to the Crown

"I will instruct you and teach you in the way you should go; I will counsel you and watch over you"

Psalms 32:8 (NLT)

My dad was a salesman for Baxter Pharmaceuticals. His job relocated our family when I was three years old living in Ann Arbor, Michigan for two years, Orlando and Ft. Lauderdale Florida for four years, and Knoxville, Tennessee for five years. When my dad's company was bought out, we moved back to Williamson which was a small coal mining town nestled in the mountains of West Virginia. This is where all my cousins and family had lived for generations.

Every Christmas we would celebrate at my Papaw and Granny's house. This was a family tradition where the entire family including my three aunts, three uncles and thirteen first cousins would come to celebrate together. Walking into my grandparents' home for every holiday celebration, I remember the sweet smell of blackberry cobbler topped with vanilla ice cream. Fun fact: The research states you pick your perfume based on scents reminiscent of childhood memories.

Every time I spray my Trish McEvoy perfume with blackberry/vanilla scent, it takes me back to days gone by.

My Papaw who always smelled like tobacco would welcome us at the door with a hug, then we would write our names down on a piece of paper to play the lottery. Whoever got picked, received a cash price of one hundred dollars from my Uncle Truman. There was always a lot of laughter and joy in my grandparents' home. Before the Christmas meal, my Papaw would always say a blessing over the food and our entire family. It was so powerful. I know those prayers have protected and guided me throughout my life.

My favorite part of Christmas dinner was my granny's biscuits and gravy. My granny was only 4'11" but commanded the room and her talents for cooking, painting, and sewing were exceptional.

I had two sets of grandparents that I loved with all my heart. My mom's parents who I just mentioned, my Granny Hazel and Papaw Tom. They would take me to their Baptist Church in Matewan, West Virginia. To get to this Church was a mountainous journey but worth the ride. On my way, I recall many coal trucks passing us on these country roads. I remember the banjo player and my Papaw singing his favorite song in the choir, "The Old Rugged Cross" in his deep, rich voice. The preacher was genuine and opened my heart to the love of God. I remember kneeling at the cross and asking Jesus into my heart at this tiny country church.

My other set of grandparents Edna and Kelly Griffith lived in South Charleston, West Virginia. This was an hour from Williamson. We would visit them every Easter and take my grandmother to her favorite restaurant, Bob Evan's. My grandfather was incredibly quiet, as a young man, he was striking like my father. After years of working tirelessly, he retired from Union Carbide. I remember him sitting in his La-Z-Boy watching TV. My grandmother was full of energy, she was elegant and beautiful. She always wore her pearls and was ready for any occasion. They lived in a two-bedroom apartment. My dad told me that during the great depression my grandmother had saved all her change to pay for this apartment that ended up being their forever home.

Both sets of grandparents had lived through the great depression, were both married for over sixty years and devoted to faith and family. They taught me a lot about the Bible and showed me that commitment, honesty, and perseverance are the road to the true crown.

Chapter 9

Bestower of Crowns

"You will also be a crown of beauty in the hand of the Lord, and a royal diadem in the hand of your God"

Isaiah 62:3 (NASB)

As a little girl, I can still remember playing with Barbies. I loved dressing them up in different outfits, styling their hair, and doing their makeup. Speaking of the movie *Barbie*, what happened to Ken? Barbie without Ken, not in my book. I have a lifetime of role models including both grandfathers, my father, father-in-law, husband, uncles, brothers, brother in laws and son supporting the evidence that men are leaders; educated, chivalrous, and strong. Of course, that was just a movie!

And back to the crown, I loved everything to do with beauty and fashion. I also loved dance, taking jazz, ballet, and tap. These interests led me to compete in my first pageant.

At the age of seventeen, I got a flyer in the mail to register for the fair pageant being held in my grandparents' hometown. This was a historic part of Mingo County and another coal mining town in the mountains of West Virginia, thirty minutes from Williamson.

Attempts to unionize by coal miners in the 1920's inspired the 1987 movie *Matewan*.

This pageant had been around since the 1940's. The pageant was called "Miss Magnolia Fair." May the fairest of them all win the crown. My pretty mother had competed in this pageant as a teenager and now my sister was going to compete. At the age of seventeen, my sister Wendy won the coveted title of Miss Magnolia Fair.

Now I was ready to win this crown. I asked my mom if I could compete in this pageant. She was hesitant because "what if" I did not win the crown? She wanted to protect me from heartache. But I was willing to take the risk. I never thought I was beautiful. I had short hair, and my sister had the most beautiful long hair. I prayed every day for long hair. I permed my hair a lot because that was the style in the 80's. Looking back, I am sure it damaged my hair and caused it not to grow longer. But I thought to myself, *I am tall, slender and have a pretty face.* I thought I was pretty enough. Maybe I could win the crown, so I got approval from my anxious mom and signed up.

We were judged on three categories: Bathing suit, gown and onstage question. I remember standing on the stage and the host asking the question, "Who is my favorite Singer?" I said Rick Springfield! Who did not love Rick Springfield ("Jessie's Girl")? He was an actor on the soap opera *General Hospita*l and a teen heartthrob. Fun fact: my fabulous friend Kathy Keller and I went to see this legend at a 2019 Concert in Charlestown, West Virginia. In my eyes, even at the age of seventy, he was still an American Idol.

On this stage, I remember wearing a pink ruffle one piece for the bathing suit competition and a pink princess dress for the Gown competition. When the judges finished scoring, all the contestants were waiting to hear the winner. Looking at all these girls, everyone was young and beautiful. How would the judges decide the winner? I had big dreams of one day competing on the Miss America Stage and being a supermodel like my favorite, Cindy Crawford. When they called my name, I felt this was a gift from God. At this moment in time, I was too young to understand the power of the appointed and anointed crown.

After winning this title, I was put on the front page of our local newspaper in Williamson, West Virginia. There were other exciting perks such as being selected to appear in our town parade wearing my sash and crown. The song "Little Red Corvette" by Prince was at the top of the charts that year and the perfect song because my high school boyfriend was the owner of a little red corvette and the chauffeur for my reign. I met Randy a year before at a Williamson High School football game. I was a majorette, and he had come to watch the game. I remember wearing my sparkly sequin leotard, twirling my baton, and seeing this handsome boy in the bleachers smiling at me. He was striking standing 6'7" with red wavy hair. He was a basketball star for Matewan High School which was our rival team. He was my first real boyfriend. It was puppy love, sweet and innocent. I was his princess, and he was my prince.

Chapter 10

Miss Mingo County

"So, whether you eat or drink, or whatever you do, do all to the glory of God."

1 Corinthians 10:31 (NIV)

My senior year in high school, I signed up to compete in another pageant. This was a local pageant that would lead to a bigger stage. I was still very innocent. I did not realize how this pageant would affect my life. A lot of people believe pageantry is not important, but let's ask Arnold Schwarzenegger what he thinks. His 2023 documentary, *Arnold*, showcases his rise to fame from a small town in Austria, competing in body building pageants that led him to become a Hollywood icon and prominent political figure.

Competing in this pageant was going to take a lot more preparation. My majorette coach helped prepare a jazz routine to "Eye of the Tiger." This song was played in *Rocky III*, the biggest blockbuster movie of the year starring Sylvester Stallone.

My grandmother Hazel was a very talented seamstress and sewed a life size dummy and red silk boxers for my routine. The stage was set up with a boxing ring. I did my jazz routine pretending to be the world champion, looking the part, wearing red boxing gloves to match. As the music started, I came out punching to the upbeat music. At the end of the performance, I punched the life size dummy into the audience. It was an electrifying ending to this winning performance ending in a standing ovation from the crowd.

At the time, I did not realize the theme of this movie would be my life story, the underdog overcoming and winning the crown against all odds many years later. In the 2024 documentary *Sly*, writer, producer, and actor, of this iconic role, Sylvester Stallone stated "nothing punches harder than life."

At this specific pageant, young women from each town in Mingo County came to Williamson to compete for the title of Miss Mingo County. This pageant was connected to the Junior Miss Pageant System. This organization had competitions at the county, state, and the national level. The judging was based on scholastics, fitness, poise, and appearance.

That night standing on that stage, I wondered if I would be beautiful, smart, and talented enough to win the crown again. Looking into the audience, I saw my mom waiting to hear the judge's selection. When they announced the winner, I saw joy in my mom's face. I had now won my second crown as "Miss Mingo County Junior Miss." I also won ribbons for excellence in physical fitness, poise, and appearance. With these two crowns, I believed God was leading me to my destiny.

Chapter 11

Junior Miss Pageant

"Trust the Lord with all thine heart;
and lean not unto thine own understanding"

Proverbs 3:5 (NIV)

As the reigning Miss Mingo County, I would now compete at the state level in a month. After taking home two titles in a row, I was full of confidence, and I believed I could surely seize the third crown. I did not realize that at the next level, the competition would be so fierce. This state pageant focused on beauty and brains. The judging was based on an interview, swimsuit, and evening gown just like the Miss America System.

What's remarkable about winning two consecutive crowns is that I was never officially trained to become a beauty queen. I thought you walked on stage looking pretty, answered the questions and smiled. I was so naïve. I would realize soon enough that beauty pageants were a sport. Many girls prepared from kindergarten. Parents spent thousands to hire coaches specializing in walking, dance, public speaking, interview, dress, hair, and makeup. This was big business.

I became aware during the state pageant interview that I was unprepared. When they asked me about my future career, I said I would like to be a fashion designer. But when they asked me how I was going to change the world, just like Sandra Bullock in the movie *Miss Congeniality*, I did not have the correct response to earn the highest marks. I had very little life experience and did not know the answer at that time. I did not smile during the evening gown competition; the bright lights and the judges made me overwhelmed.

When they announced the winner, I believed that was the end of my pageant days. I believe this was also my mom's dream from many years gone by. I was heartbroken and disappointed. That night I buried that dream and thought I would never look back. My mom and I would not talk about pageantry and the crown for thirty-six years.

Chapter 12

College Years

"And do not be conformed to this world, but be transformed by the renewing of your mind, that you may prove what is good and acceptable and perfect will of God"

Romans 12:2 (KJV)

Most people love college, but I was from a small town and very sheltered, not ready for this wild ride. I had never had a sip of alcohol. I was a Christian girl and loved Jesus. The first day I went to college, let's just say there were many bottles of beer. Every social activity included alcohol. How was I supposed to study?

Another problem was that I had no direction. When I left for college, my parents encouraged me to be a teacher or a nurse. I did not want to go into those fields. Even though both professions are honorable, I was too young to understand. I was looking for the glamorous life just like Sheila E. who found her Prince. I knew I loved fashion and was interested in pursuing this stylish career and partying like it's 1999.

My sister was an Alpha Phi, so my parents encouraged me to join this sorority. Because of my sister, I was considered a legacy. A legacy is automatically chosen because of family. Looking back on this decision, it was a joyous time, and I was grateful to have the love of many sisters and make lifelong friends.

Going to the football games was one of the highlights of my time at WVU. And attending the football formal with a guy named Chris was my first Oscar moment. He had black curly hair, was six feet tall, and muscular. My girlfriend who lived down the hall fixed me up. Her boyfriend was also a football player and believe me these boys received star treatment. I wore a gorgeous emerald gown, and he wore a black tux. Walking into the venue, cameras flashing, I thought we were on the red carpet.

I genuinely believed there was a flame. I guess he did not feel the spark. After that night, he never called again. This was the beginning of many heartbreaks. He sent a friend request forty years later, which is an interesting fact. I accepted with pleasure; this piqued my interest. He was divorced yet still attractive; I was now blissfully wed.

Trying out for the WVU calendar during sophomore year was another thrilling opportunity. Obviously, there was not a lot of studying going on. Back to the context, this was a highly sought-after title. Twelve girls would be selected by the appointed judges, one for each month. Even *Sports Illustrated* came to the campus to choose a cover girl for the upcoming spring issue. My sister and I were destined to try out as the previous summer my sister won Miss Hawaiian Tropic and I won Miss Grand Strand.

Don't you know out of more than five hundred college females, my sister was chosen to be one of the calendar girls. She was meant to be famous and is currently a well-known reporter. She is also the author of the book *You Didn't Miss It!* and *A Prize to be Won*. I was ecstatic for her success but would continue to believe that "destiny" belongs to the underdogs, knowing one day I would recapture the crown.

Chapter 13

A Man's World

"In all thy ways acknowledge him and he will direct thy paths"

Proverbs 3:6 (KJV)

I was having too much fun at WVU. Too much socializing and not enough studying. My GPA got so low I had to transfer schools, ending up at Marshall University. They did not have fashion merchandising, but I successfully graduated with a B.A. in speech communication.

After graduating, I was still unsure what my future career would be. I always thought I would meet the man of my dreams in college, get married, and have children.

This obviously was not God's plan for my life. But what was God's plan? My entire college life was one big party. There was no time for God. I lived in the world and the motto was "If it feels good, do it!" Unfortunately, as a Christian girl, this did not bring me any happiness or fulfillment.

Luckily, my mom and dad bought a condo in Charleston, South Carolina on the Isle of Palms. My sister, who had graduated two years prior, landed a job as a reporter. I packed my bags and happily left Huntington, West Virginia.

Looking for a job with a degree in communication was like finding a needle in a haystack. I was very determined to find the perfect job and applied for a sales recruiter position for Rutledge College in Charleston, South Carolina. My duties were to call people from the phone book, make an appointment and have them enroll in an associate program. I worked at this job for two years, ten hours a day and made $11,000.00 per year. I never was an "A" student, but I had an incredible work ethic. I was the number one salesperson for this Community College.

My dad was in sales and was the hardest working man I knew. He taught my sisters and brothers that honesty is the best policy. When I was young, he told us a story about his friend who worked for Coco-Cola. This friend had a great job and made a lot of money. He was caught stealing but because the company believed he was an honorable man; they gave him one more chance. He stole again, after that, they fired him. My dad cautioned us about his friend's dishonesty, as he lost his job and his family. This story has stuck with me my whole life.

After two years, I applied at another college and received a raise, now making $14,000 a year. I had other friends in pharmaceutical sales making $60,000 a year. Why did I set my goals so low? I did not feel confident enough to apply for a pharmaceutical sales position. But now looking back, that would have been much easier than selling the intangible associate degree. The good news is this job set me up for many future successes in my life.

During this time, I met a guy named Tom at a college bar in downtown Charleston. He was a senior at the Citadel, a prestigious military college in town. He was also the running back for the football team and was getting his degree in political science. I remember the moment our eyes met, and he walked over to me. He was using crunches from a football injury. I believed at first glance that he was the man of my dreams. Tom had brown wavy hair, dark eyes, and a football player physique.

In every fairytale, the prince is charming. For my birthday, he bought me a diamond crown necklace and for Christmas he sent me a dozen long stemmed roses. He seemed like the perfect boyfriend and future husband. After dating for a year, he graduated, applied to law schools, and got accepted at Ohio University. As you know, my mom always hoped I would be a lawyer. I never had an interest in that field. Like I mentioned in previous chapters, I have many uncles and cousins that are lawyers. My baby brothers would also go to one of the finest colleges in the country and become attorneys one day. I was happy my boyfriend wanted to be in this prestigious field. He would be very successful and make a fabulous income so we could get married and live happily ever after.

Unfortunately, this is not how the story would end! He got accepted to Ohio University and broke up with me on Halloween. I remember with the innocence of a child; the breakup was so unexpected. We were getting ready to go to a Halloween Party. I was dressed like Juliet, but this was not my Romeo.

In my family history, Johnson "Johnse" Hatfield fell in love with Roseanna, the youngest daughter of Randolph McCoy. This was a forbidden love just like Romeo and Juliet. Because she was a McCoy, Devil Anse refused to let them marry. She was with child and moved in with the Hatfield Clan. Then realizing there would be no betrothal, before giving birth, she moved in with her aunt. Johnse ended up marrying her cousin two years later. It was devastating and they say she died of a broken heart. If you believe in synchronicities, Roseanna McCoy was born on March 21st. This is also my husband's birthday.

Back to my tragic love story, he said he would love me forever. My heart was broken once again. My entire twenties, I felt hopeless and unloved because of this breakup. I sincerely felt I almost died from heartbreak just like Roseanna McCoy. I knew Tom was going to be successful but never in my wildest dreams did I think he would have a net worth of $72 million dollars. He would reach out to me many years later, it was too late; I had found true love.

But back to the story, I was trying to find love and marriage. Times were changing and men were not interested in getting married so early in life. A lot of women were becoming professionals also, but I was old fashioned. I did not care about a career, I just wanted to find love. Where was that love that I was so desperately searching for?

After the breakup, feeling so depressed, I quit my job and decided to be a waitress. I got a job at a restaurant called California Dreaming. Speaking of dreams, I believe God wants us to dream big. Looking back, I realize I was dreaming too small.

At the restaurant, there were a lot of young people like me in between jobs and searching for the perfect career. I made a lot more money waiting tables than as a recruiter. After a year as a server and mending my broken heart, I was ready to go back home to the mountains of West Virginia.

Chapter 14

Country Roads

"Your word is a lamp to my feet and a light for my path."

Psalms 119:105 (NASB)

Driving down those winding roads, I was still young and wild. Was I ready to surrender my life to God, the cross and the plans he had for me? I felt lost. Where was God taking me.

Now back in Charleston, West Virginia, my sister had changed TV stations. She and I were roommates once again. This is also where my brothers attended high school, to get the finest education a big city has to offer. Fun fact, Jennifer Garner, America Actress, best known for her iconic role in the movie *13 Going on 30* and former wife to A lister Ben Affleck attended the same school and was a couple grades ahead of them.

Now the search was on to find the perfect job. I researched the papers and interviewed with a company called Hamilton Computer Products. They were looking for an instructor to teach basic computer classes. I had no experience in this field, but they believed in me, and I was hired and learned quickly. I was then required to recruit companies to come to the business and teach the classes. My first class was a group of six people. This company was part of The Secret Service located in West Virginia. I assumed they would all be driving black BMW's, Aston Martins and be debonair, dangerous, and beautiful. I was still single and ready to meet my James Bond. To my dismay when they arrived, they were all happily married. A couple in the class were Christian and invited me to their Nazarene Church. I was in desperate need of direction and gladly went the next Sunday. When I stepped into that church, I felt the presence of God just like many years before at my grandparent's country church where I had accepted Jesus into my heart. All these years from eighteen to twenty-four, I had forgotten God, but God was calling me back into His loving arms.

I worked at Hamilton Computer Products for a year before I had an opportunity to work for the West Virginia Legislature. My Uncle Truman, being a State Senator, referred me for a secretary position for Senator Mark Manchin, brother to Senator Joe Manchin. This experience was not just another day at the office. Many years later, Joe Manchin would become a United States Senator and one of the most powerful men in the country. I worked two consecutive years for the West Virginia Legislature. The session would meet three months out of the year. The burning question was, what was God's plan for my life and where was the crown?

Chapter 15

Graduate School & The Dangerous Liaisons

*"But seek ye first the Kingdom of God and
all these things will be given to you"*

Mathew 6:33 (KJV)

I decided to go back to school and get a specialized degree. I picked a Master of Arts in English/Education. Teaching was a respectable field, so I started taking classes and would drive from Charleston to Huntington twice a week.

I ran into Tristan; I knew from undergrad. He had black curly hair and olive skin reminding me of John Travolta from the movie, "Saturday Night Fever." When we looked at each other all the heartbreak from my previous love faded away.

I really enjoyed my classes and was excited to learn something new and improve myself. Now that I was dating Tristan, I felt alive again. I had never met anyone as charming and fun. He loved rollercoasters, movies, dinner, and dancing. When we were together, I was the only one for him. When we were apart, he had endless trysts.

Tristan did not drink but unfortunately, he did drugs. I did not realize this until after six months of dating. The problem with drugs is that they are very easy to get addicted to. I did not know what drug he was using but realized this was not the first time. After I found out about this problem, I tried to help him. I asked him to go to church and we would go together. He would try to stop doing drugs, but the addiction got worse. Then he needed the drugs every day, so he started selling drugs to make money to get more drugs. At this point, we had been on and off for a year and I knew we had to break up. Now the FBI had called me asking questions. Even though I was an innocent victim, I knew this guy was committing a crime. Unfortunately, he was hurting himself more than anyone else. I broke up with him after this incident. Even from the beginning I realized, this was not love, this was an unhealthy obsession.

A week after the breakup, I went out to a restaurant on a double date with my best friend Kim Ward, future husband Chris and his friend Rich to mend my broken heart. We were having such a good time, and my date seemed like a real gentleman. Then in an instant, my ex-Tristan came over and hit Rich over the head with a beer bottle. There was blood everywhere. I was in shock. Everyone jumped up and defended Rich and a big fight broke out. This guy had to go to the emergency room but thank the Lord, he only needed a couple stitches. God had protected this guy. Even more significant is God had protected me because I should have been the target. I realized then; God had a bigger plan for my life. I could not help him change his life, but I could change mine. He was the ruler of his kingdom, and I must be the ruler of my realm and go find my crown.

It was a small college town, and everyone knew I was dating the wrong guy. Why did I set my standards so low? I never felt worthy, pretty enough, or smart enough. After two years of this rollercoaster ride, I was ready to get off!

I did my student teaching and was going to stay to take my final exam in the summer. But then I believe God intervened. My sister Nancy, who had graduated, was now living in Raleigh, North

Carolina. She was a kindergarten teacher and like me, she was a free spirit. Teaching was not our dream job. She told me that a small startup company, Midway Airlines, was hiring flight attendants. I had been waiting to apply for a flight attendant job but there had been a freeze on hiring for many years.

The next day I drove to Raleigh with my resume in hand. I went straight to human resources and asked to speak to the person hiring flight attendants. The secretary said I would have to mail my resume to this address. I did not have time to wait, I had been searching all my life for the perfect career.

Since the day I lost the state title, I had been through incredible heartache and rejection. I went outside of human resources and prayed for God to help me.

A young guy who worked on the ramp came over to me and asked if I needed help. I truly believe this guy was an angel from heaven. I told him my story and he said follow me. He took me past the secretary to the lady hiring flight attendants. I got the job that day. God is faithful.

The royal adventure was about to begin!

Chapter 16

A Child is Born

*"Before I formed you in the womb, I knew you.
Before you were born, I set you apart"*

Jeremiah 1:5 (GW)

At forty-one and newly married, my dream was now to have a family. I had been married for three months and had come home from a three-day trip as a flight attendant. I had an excruciating headache. I had never felt so exhausted or tired in my life.

Could it be? I made an appointment the next day with the OBGYN. I said I was newlywed and forty-one and really hoping I was pregnant. She took a blood test, and it came back negative. She told me I was probably too old to get pregnant. Then she gave me a script to get my eggs checked. I did not realize they had this state-of-the-art procedure. I knew that it was possible to get pregnant later in life because my mom had had her fifth child at thirty-eight. And that was many years before. To be able to get pregnant at any stage in life is a miracle. I believe life begins at conception and even though the test came back negative, I knew in my heart that God had done something miraculous.

Two weeks later, I was still feeling unusual, so I went to the Dollar Store and got a pregnancy test. When I got home, I took the test, and it came back positive. By the grace of God, I was pregnant!! When my husband came home from work that day, I told him the joyful news. We were both in amazement at God's wondrous plan.

I went back to work the next week and during the trip, I had another excruciating headache. When I arrived home, I had terrible cramps. I almost lost the baby. The doctor said I must be on bed rest for two weeks. I was so anxious at first and got on my knees and prayed. I was not a career girl. My whole life, even from when I was a little girl, all I ever wanted was to get married and have a family. I told God if this child survived, I would prepare it for great and mighty things.

After the two-week point, I was allowed to go back to my normal routine, but I was told not to fly again until the end of the three-month period. At sixteen weeks, we were able to find out the gender. It was so exciting to see my beautiful baby on the sonogram. We heard the heartbeat and found out we were having a boy. In a world where many women use abortion as birth control, as a Christian, my eyes were wide open to the masterpiece that God had created.

I ended up taking the leave as a flight attendant to protect my son. For the first few months, I looked like I had gained a little weight. The following months, I looked like I was carrying a basketball. I loved being pregnant with my first child knowing he was healthy and safe. I never felt happier and more beautiful. The sky was bluer, music was sweeter, and food was yummier!

Then at the nine-month mark, on the predicted day, I got up to go to the bathroom and my water broke, the baby was on the way. I woke up my husband and told him it was time to go. I was so nervous about having this baby, but nature was about to take its course. I started having contractions. At first, they were not painful but by the time we got to the hospital, it was time for the epidural.

After pushing for eight hours, the baby was ready to be delivered. Everything seemed to be going perfectly. The doctor decided to use the vacuum to guide the baby out but then the baby's shoulder got stuck. Not only was the shoulder stuck but the umbilical cord got wrapped around his neck. It was now an emergency. They could not do a c-section either. At this point, everyone in the room was in a panic. There was very little time left before my son would run out of oxygen. They were doing a procedure where they tried to break the baby's shoulder. This did not work either. Then they gave me a double episiotomy.

Any pregnancy after the age of forty is considered high risk. My son's life was precious, and I was willing to die for him to survive. I was holding my cross necklace and praying during this time believing God was going to help me deliver a healthy baby. After this procedure, the doctor was able to successfully deliver. I believe God was in the room that day. My doctor who was also a woman had had the same birth experience as me, so she knew exactly what to do in this emergency situation.

Once my son was delivered, I thought my husband was going to faint. My baby was a pale blue color. They were slapping his back, but he was not crying. By this time, I was screaming and saying to my baby, "I love you!" over and over. I kept telling my husband to say this also. During my pregnancy, I read many articles about giving birth. One article said when a baby is in distress, if it hears the parents voice, miracles can happen. We needed a miracle. After what seemed like eternity, he started crying and it was one of the happiest moments of my life.

He was a miracle child. He had escaped death twice already. I knew God had great plans for this little king!!

Chapter 17

New York State of Mind

"Arise, walk about the land through its length and breadth; for I will give it to you"

Genesis 13:17 (NASB)

Being a stay-at-home mom for twelve years to make it to one of the most prestigious stages in the world was not a coincidence.

After winning Mrs. DC America 2020, I went to compete on the Mrs. America Stage in March of 2021. I was holding on to this dream to win the national crown. I knew I was older, but with age comes elegance. Unfortunately, I had never competed at this level and the National Level of competition was comparable to competing for the Olympics.

The girls on this stage were not just younger, but a lot of these ladies had been formally trained since childhood. I believed my interview would get top scores because my platform was mentoring young girls to become future leaders through the Girl Scouts of the United States of America.

What I learned more than anything on the Mrs. America Stage, is the "Walk" is everything! I was not prepared for this, the "Walk" was similar to a dance and every contestant had a different style. I learned that week why the top runway models in the world were making millions. I was ready to set my sights on a higher calling than Mrs. America.

Chapter 18

The Gift

"Behold, children are a heritage from the Lord, the fruit of the womb a reward."

Psalms 127:3 (ESV)

I really wanted a sibling for my son. I had been so blessed to have two brothers and two sisters. I loved my big family and cherished the times we would get together for holiday celebrations. My dad was an only child and he said he was best friends was his dog, Blackie. My dad had Blackie from the time he was one until he was eighteen. When his dog died, it was like losing his brother. I did not want my son to have this same experience.

When my son was eight months old, we decided to try for another baby and see if God would make another miracle happen. After two months, I was pregnant again. With God's favor, I was going to have another baby at the age of forty-three!!

My second pregnancy was easy. I had no complications. But I did have some major differences this time around. At twelve weeks, we found out we were having a girl. This is called a millionaire family and I felt like a million dollars!!

They say when you are pregnant with a boy, he gives you beauty and when you are pregnant with a girl, she takes your beauty. I believe this statement!! I was beautiful when I was pregnant with my son but with my daughter, I looked exhausted.

The practice I was going to did not perform c-sections. I was getting worried because I had so many complications with my first pregnancy. Then at eight months, they cancelled my appointment because the office had overbooked. I decided to switch practices at nine months. The new practice did an ultrasound. My baby weighed eight pounds. They suggested I have a c-section because they were worried my baby would be too big and I might have complications with my delivery.

We scheduled the c-section and the day we went in for delivery my water broke. My daughter was ready to come into the world. My husband was allowed to be in the room for the c-section. I am not sure how he got up the courage after the last delivery. The doctor numbed me before the c-section. I do not know all the medical terms, but I was awake, and I could feel them cutting me. At this point, it became an emergency, and they gave laughing gas that knocked me out.

My daughter had jet black hair and olive skin. Both my husband and I have light skin and light brown hair. If I had not had a c-section, I would have thought they gave me the wrong baby. She looked Italian or American-Indian. The good news is my husband has Italian descendants and I have American-Indian descendants, so she was a mix of many generations before us. We knew we had an exotic beauty beyond what we could have imagined.

This baby was not shy. She screamed so loud and made her voice heard being the opposite of our son. A princess was born.

Chapter 19

Everything that Glitters Isn't Gold

*"There is gold, and an abundance of jewels;
But the lips of knowledge are a more precious thing."*

Proverbs 20:15 (NASB)

My husband's company was closing his department, after working for them for twenty-five years he was ready to take a year off. I had been home for ten years with the kids cooking and cleaning. I was ready to go out into the work force.

Loving fashion and design, I found a job at a Swarovski, this global company originated in Austria, founded by Daniel Swarovski. His magnificent machine mastered the cutting of the crystal, making it appear to resemble a real diamond.

Starting at $11 dollars an hour, seemed hard to imagine since a babysitter goes for $15 dollars per hour. My resume clearly confirmed I was more than qualified for this job. I had worked over forty different customer service jobs and flew domestic/international for twelve years traveling to over twenty different countries. The manager said because I had been out of the workforce for ten years, I needed to work a year and then meet the sales quota for each month. After a year, I would be able to qualify for a raise.

The perks of working at this store was getting fifty percent off on the jewelry. Everyone who had a birthday got a beautiful gift that year. I also met two forever friends, Ruby and Cheryl, at this job. During our breaks, we would write quotes from different movies to encourage and keep our dreams alive. In one of my favorite inspirational movies by Will Smith, *Pursuit of Happyness*, he is speaking to his young son to encourage him. He quotes, "You got a dream, you got to protect it. Don't ever let somebody tell you, you can't do something. If you want something, go get it."

After the year, having achieved the sales quota, I met with the manager to discuss a raise. But shockingly, she said that no one was getting a raise that year. I sold thousands of dollars of jewelry, and I was not worthy enough to be paid more than $11 dollars an hour. The other employees with less experience were earning $15 dollars an hour. I believe I was worth more and gave my two weeks' notice.

Now I was going to pursue my real dream of modeling. When I was working at Swarovski, people would come in and tell me I should be the face of this brand. The model that year, Miranda Kerr, was also a Victoria Secret Model. This was a foreshadowing of future dreams, and this set the stage for my future goals. With my husband by my side, we spent several thousand dollars on modeling pictures but none of these were picture perfect. I was truly feeling defeated and then my sister Wendy contacted me with great news. She met a lady who was a NY model at an elegant affair. Immediately, my sister inquired about a photographer, the model had referred David Kaptein. I believe this was a divine appointment.

I called David and ended up speaking to his wife, Lena, for over an hour. They lived twenty minutes outside of NYC, were both models in their twenties and met on a shoot in Paris. How romantic. He was the photographer, and she was the hair and makeup team. I expressed my dreams of being a model. After receiving my pictures, Lena confirmed that she and her husband could help make my dreams come true just like the 80's classic by Daryl Hall & John Oates.

I made an appointment, my husband and kids got in the car, and we drove to New York City looking for the crown.

Chapter 20

The Greatest Love

"So now faith, hope, and love abide, these three; but the greatest of these is love"

1 Corinthians 13:13 (ESV)

After all the tears, heartache and loneliness of thirty-eight years, my prayers were about to be answered.

I had moved to Philadelphia and thought I would never go back to DC. Where were the educated, handsome, and godly men? I believe they were all taken or married.

I decided I must make a change; I might be alone for the rest of my life but at least I was going to have fun.

I transferred to Philadelphia to fly International. It was an exciting time. My favorite destination was Paris. As a flight attendant for US Airways, the company would fly people to their destination. Then the crew would go from the airport to the hotel. One of the perks was the hotels were in the city and we could walk to everything. We would usually have a day to explore and enjoy the sights. Many of the crew members had been flying this route for years, so they would not be interested in exploring the city. When we stayed in Paris, I would walk to the Champs Elysée, go shopping at the beautiful boutiques and sit at the Parisian Cafe's having coffee and pastries. The French people were always very welcoming and being alone a lot, I always felt safe and at home in this beautiful setting.

Some of the other destinations I loved were Spain, Germany, Ireland, Italy, and England. I realized this was not just a job but an educational experience. I learned so much about other cultures, their history, language, music, and cuisine.

I had been living this regal life for a year but unexpectantly it was about to change. Every year, depending on seniority, the flight attendants would submit to fly international. If you could speak another language, you would be at the top of the list. I was not a speaker but now I had eight years with the company. I resubmitted my request and was approved for another year!

By a twist of fate, my paperwork got lost in the shuffle. The company informed me that I must transfer back to DC until my paperwork was found or I was to resubmit and wait for an opening. I was so frustrated by this news but happy to have a wonderful friend in DC. I called my most fabulous friend Kathy Keller. She said I could sleep on her couch for a month. The month turned into three months. Instead of sleeping on her couch, I got the bed. Somehow, I charmed her into letting me sleep in her room. She is the one of the sweetest and most generous people I have ever met.

Kathy and I were both single in the city. We tried meeting guys at church, bars and dating sites. To no avail, it never worked out. I do not want to be braggadocious, but Kathy and I were both pretty. Unfortunately, though, we were horrible at picking the right guy, so we always ended up with a broken heart. Kathy encouraged me to try Match.com one more time. She said we could both do it together, and maybe this time we would both find true love.

At the end of the three months, it looked hopeless until I got a match. This guy emailed me and sent his name, resume and picture.

The picture was a little blurry, but he was tall, muscular and it looked like he had a cute face. He was also close to my age and had never been married. Was this too good to be true? I sent him an email back and we planned to meet at Starbucks the next day.

I remember wearing a pink top and black pants. I felt like *Pretty Woman* and was hoping this was my Richard Gere. As I walked into the Starbucks, I did not see anyone that looked like him. Then I realized there was an outside patio. I walked outside and saw a guy sitting by himself. I walked up to him and shyly asked if his name was Paul. He stood up 6 foot 4, muscular, handsome, and my heart melted. He shook my hand and said, "Yes, I am Paul." When his hand touched mine, I felt the greatest love; after all these years, I had found my prince charming.

All this time, I had been waiting, searching, and praying. God's timing is perfect, the romance continued for two enchanted years. Then at the age of forty we got married in Washington DC. My husband was eighteen months younger than me. I remember my dad saying he was surprised Paul was interested in an older woman. Paul's mom was eighteen months older than his dad. And if you do not believe in God's plan, Paul's dad's name was "Jean" and his mom's name is "Anne." My name is JeanAnne. God's royal plan.

Chapter 21

The Cross and the Crown

"As he spoke to me the spirit entered me and set me on my feet; and I heard him speaking to me"

Ezekiel 2:2 (ESV)

I never realized the crown had anything to do with the cross until the moment before they called my name as Mrs. DC America 2020. I literally heard God speak! He said in an audible voice, "You are anointed an appointed." Then the announcer called my name as the winner. When I won the crown, I had hundreds of people congratulating me. This was not just a beauty pageant, I was now on a major stage and God wanted me to shine my light in the darkness, have influence and help others.

Before I won the crown, behind the scenes, I had been a faithful servant to the Lord since I was 13. Then I rededicated my life again getting baptized and born again at the Nazarene Church at the age of twenty-six in Charleston, WV. At this Church, on that stage they completely immersed me in the water. During this moment of the anointing, I thought back to my great, great, great Uncle Devil Anse. He did not have a crown, but he was said to be a "leader of men." He was also baptized and totally immersed in the water of Island Creek and gave his life to the Lord after the feud ended at the age of seventy-two. Folklore says he still had a loaded gun in his pocket, but he was forever changed after being baptized by his best friend, Uncle Dyke Garrett, in the heavenly mountain springs of West Virgina.

I truly believe he had an invisible crown.

Chapter 22

My Daughter

"And our daughters will be like pillars carved to adorn a palace"

Psalms 144:12 (NIV)

From the moment I saw this exotic beauty, she melted my heart. My husband and I decided to name her KellyAnne. My father's name is Kelly, and his father was also Kelly. There is power in a name, and I wanted her to have a strong and powerful name. Kelly means "Warrior Princess" and Anne means "Grace." This was very befitting of my little queen.

From the time she was a baby, my daughter would not let anyone else hold her. Every time someone else tried to pick her up, she would scream. Even my husband was not allowed to hold her. My daughter and I ended up hugging each other for six years until she was too big to hold. Before I met my husband, I had traveled the world looking for love and now I had unconditional love. This hug healed me from many years of feeling unlovable.

As a little girl, my daughter had many talents. One of her talents she loved was to write stories. She would make booklets and staple the papers together. She would then write the title of the book on the cover. Her writing was so exceptional we even checked with a publisher about getting her stories put into a book.

Several years later when KellyAnne was nine, I decided to pursue modeling and acting. To submit to this agency, I had to have a monologue, so my daughter wrote a thirty second script for me. My role was "mom." I am not sure how she even knew what a monologue was, but she was determined to help me get on with this agency. I believe she is a creative genius. Then I had to pick a song, so I chose to sing, "Take Me Home, Country Roads." I wasn't a professional singer; I was similar to Adam Sandler in the comedy/romance *The Wedding Singer*. Karaoke, anyone?

Linda Townsend Management was the first agency I signed with that believed with me in my modeling/acting dreams and was ready to take a risk with a stay-at-home mom that was over the age of fifty. Interesting fact: Linda Townsend is also a queen.

Chapter 23

The Sheriff

> *"To the one who is victorious and does my will to the end,*
> *I will give authority over the nations"*
>
> **Revelations 2:26 (NIV)**

I love the classic song by Bob Marley, "I Shot the Sheriff." This song was relevant to my life because at the age of thirteen my grandfather was the Sheriff of Mingo County. My grandfather started his career as a coal miner in the mountains of West Virginia at the age of fifteen. He worked in those treacherous mines until the age of twenty-eight. He then became a bus driver and small business owner managing a local grocery store. My grandfather also had a passion for public service. His first elected position was Constable in the Magnolia District of Mingo County. This was the first of many elected offices he would hold during his thirty-six years of public service to the citizens of Mingo County. His final race was running for office and winning the prestigious title of "Sheriff" at the age of sixty. He was the first person to win the race for two consecutive terms. My grandfather reigned as Sheriff of Mingo County for eight years and retired at the age of sixty-eight.

My grandfather was also a devoted member and one of the baritone singers in the choir at Matewan Baptist Church. I remember as a little girl, sitting in the pew with my Granny listening to him sing at the beginning of the service. Besides my dad, he was the most magnetic person I have ever met, and his angelic voice commanded the atmosphere.

The day before I competed for Mrs. DC America 2020, my daughter and I went to Hobby Lobby. This was a Christian owned arts and crafts store. We loved walking around this store. My daughter loved to make jewelry and paint. She also loved to sew and had recently gotten a sewing machine for Christmas. I believe she had many creative talents like my grandmother. After my daughter bought material to make clothes for her barbie dolls, we went to the section with beautiful pictures. They had many plaques with Bible verses that were inspiring and uplifting.

Then, right in front of me, I saw something that took my breath away, it touched my soul and took me back in time to that Baptist Church in the exalted hills of West Virginia. It was a framed picture of musical notes that said, "I will cling to the old rugged cross and exchange it someday for a crown." This was one of my grandfather's favorite songs that he sang on Sundays in the choir.

At that moment, I knew that my grandfather was singing this beautiful melody from the Heavenly realm inspiring me to win the crown of Mrs. DC America 2020.

Chapter 24

Love from Pakistan

"For the Kingdom is the lord's and he rules over the nations"

Psalms 22:28 (NKJV)

Where is Pakistan? It is a country in South Asia. It is the fifth most populous country, with a population of over 241 million, having the second largest Muslim population in 2023. Only 1.27 percent of the population is Christian.

I had never been to this part of the world and had never met anyone from this area, but things were about to change and the Pakistani people in Washington DC would be my PR Team and promote and support me throughout my reign as Mrs. DC America 2020 and beyond.

When I was crowned Mrs. DC America 2020, I was given a public relations lady residing in Pennsylvania. I was not sure how she would represent me, but I was hoping for many opportunities to promote my platform and make a difference. Unfortunately, during 2020, almost everything was shut down due to covid. One day shortly after my crowning, I was contacted on Facebook by dashing Dr. Mobi. He is originally from Pakistan, now a sleep doctor by day and interviews celebrities by night. He asked if he could interview me on zoom., we scheduled right away and went live for the interview. After that incredible moment in 2020, I believe a lot of people listened to my story, my platform and welcomed me as the new queen.

When I won the crown, one of the prizes was a gift package for a year worth of services from my sponsored skin care specialist, owner of Nova Derm Institute. Afsheen Ather is also from Pakistan. She offers noninvasive antiaging procedures. She also creates her medical grade products, developing them through a local lab using natural ingredients. Her serum, called "fountain of youth" delivers results and is one of my favorite products. She is the queen of skincare.

I then met Cemo Basen in my acting class. He is an Instagram sensation, and he was also, surprisingly, from Pakistan. We became amazing friends in our devotion to following our dreams. When I decided to write my singles show, I chose this debonair guy "the next Johnny Depp" to be my bachelor for "Singles in the City – DC" in September of 2022.

Because of my title as Mrs. DC America 2020, I was asked to be a judge for the Miss/Mrs. Pakistan USA Pageant in 2021. This pageant inspired me to create my own pageant to highlight honorable men that are devoted to family, the community, and their profession in the DMV.

I was then referred to Tanvir Amir, who has a production company called "Star Entertainment." He is from Pakistan and a Christian. He sponsored the DJ for my Mr. DC Pageant. After this event, he asked me to be a host at the Pakistan Embassy for their Easter Celebration. It was a holy night.

I love the Pakistani/Indian culture. One of my good friends was competing for the Ms. India Crown. I decided to wear this beautiful blue chiffon dress I had bought at my favorite boutique called Signatures in Georgetown. I wasn't competing in this pageant but wanted to show up looking the part. As soon as I arrived, I met Amna

Inam. This was another moment that was going to change my life and many other upcoming models. She looked like royalty and with my crown, I realized we were meant to build the Kingdom together. She introduced herself and asked me if I would be interested in being the opener for her show in February for New York Fashion Week. I did not hesitate.

I had been waiting for this crowning moment.

Chapter 25

The Four-Legged Prince

"In his hand is the life of every creature"

Job 12:10 (NIV)

My kids were seven and nine. They were begging my husband and I for a dog. The kids started looking on a website called Petfinder. I am also a dog lover. We fell in love with so many dogs that looked like the perfect one, but we kept searching for our forever dog. Then after two months Joseph and KellyAnne found the one. He looked super cute but, in the picture, it looked like he did not have any ears. A college girl named Ally had been fostering him for two weeks. She wrote the sweetest and most heartfelt bio on this dog. She said he loved belly rubs, cuddling and he could even do tricks.

We asked my husband if we could go to Petco the following Saturday to look at the dog. I thought the dog would be located at the Petco in Manassas, but we ended up driving to Harrisonburg because that is where the foster parent Ally was located. When we finally arrived after this anticipated journey, we parked the car and looked around in front of the Petco. There were many rescue dogs waiting to be selected but I did not see that special dog. Then from the corner of my eye, I saw a dog coming towards us on a leash. He looked different than the picture. He had the most magnificent ears. This dog was a Jack Russell mix, but he had the exact coloring as my Basset hound Baxter from many years before. When he got closer, he also had the same diamond shape marking on his head.

The foster parent Ally picked him up like a baby and then unexpectantly, he jumped into my husband's arms. I have to say my husband was not a dog lover and was very startled by this aggressive animal. Actually, I believe this was a very smart dog. He wanted the leader of the pack to rescue him.

This rescue dog reminded me of my dog Baxter that I had loved so much from my childhood. Two nights before we went to look at this rescue dog, I had dreamed about him. In real life, he was a very slow dog and walked like a turtle but in the dream, he was running in a field of the greenest grass I had ever seen. I know this was heaven. Then I woke up with a smile on my face.

Back to that moment at Petco, this dog came towards me, and I started crying uncontrollably. The unconditional love from my dog Baxter came flooding back to me. He had been run over by a car when I was twelve. Remembering that moment, I lost some of my youthful innocence on that day. This dog was my answer to a childhood prayer.

This dog's name was Otto, a German name. My husband is half German, and the kids felt the German connection. They fell in love at first sight like me. We asked my husband if we could take him home, but Otto had already decided we would be his forever family. There was no turning back. The kids went into Petco with Otto and picked out his bed, collar, leash, and toy. My husband was in charge of getting the dog food. I took a picture of Otto and the kids in Petco that day; this little prince had a smile on his face. Otto knew he had found his castle.

Chapter 26

Becoming Queen

"We can make our plans, but the Lord determines our steps"

Proverbs 16:9 (NLT)

Why do so many little girls want to be princesses? I believe the crown represents beauty, honor, godliness, and a heart to serve others. I remember as a little girl watching every princess movie. Cinderella was my favorite. She had such a challenging childhood, but her kindness and inner beauty led her to the prince and the crown. In the end, she found love and became ruler of a kingdom.

For my fifth birthday, my parents had bought me a beautiful doll that I kept on my dresser until I was eighteen. This was one of my most treasured gifts. This doll had long brown hair and wore a pink gown. The most beautiful feature on this doll was the dazzling crown that adorned her head.

As I laid my head on the desk in that kindergarten room, needing a hug, I thought to myself, *one day I will be a queen and be loved and adored by many.*

Looking back in history, it is fascinating to see how these women received the crown and what they did with their titles.

The elegant Queen Noor of Jordan was originally from Washington, DC. She was also a flight attendant and met King Hussein while working for Royal Jordanian Airline. Her original name was Lisa. After marrying the King, she took Jordanian citizenship, embraced the Islamic faith, and adopted an Arabic name. Queen Noor undertook numerous philanthropic duties at home and abroad, many of which were focused on children. She established the Royal Endowment for Culture and Education, the National Music Conservatory, and the Jubilee school for gifted students.

The glamorous Grace Kelly was an American Actress. During a photocall to the Palace of Monaco for the Cannes Film Festival she met Prince Ranier who was considered the most eligible bachelor in Europe at that time. After a yearlong courtship, they married, and she became Princess Grace of Monaco. During her reign, she became involved in improving the arts by creating the Princess Grace Foundation to support local artisans.

The conventional Princess Elizabeth became Queen of England after the sudden death of her father when she was twenty-five. Before becoming queen, on her twenty-first birthday, she prepared a speech, in a radio broadcast stating to her future subjects "her whole life, whether it be long or short, shall be devoted to service." Queen Elizabeth was very devoted to God and the Church of England. Her belief and the Monarchy saw the divine connection between God and the crown. Elizabeth was christened in 1926 in a silk gown dating back to the Victorian era and baptized with water from the river Jordan.

I believe the most royal of my generation was Diana, Princess of Wales. She was a member of the British royal family and first wife of King Charles III, mother of the Princes William and Harry. Her activism and glamour made her an international icon. The wedding at St. Paul's Cathedral was a majestic sight. But the marriage did not last. She was heartbroken but she continued her queenly duties to promote love and help others on a global scale comparable to Saint Theresa. Elton John even revised his song "Candle in the Wind" for Princess Diana.

Interesting fact: I have been to Monaco (Principality), London, England, and my next stop is Jordan. Searching for the crown.

Chapter 27

The Cherry Blossom Dress

"God has made everything beautiful in its time. He has also set eternity in the human heart; yet no one can fathom what God has done from beginning to end"

Ecclesiastes 3:11 (NIV)

After winning the crown at the state level, I was now going to compete on the national stage. At this level, each contestant from each state must pick a costume to represent their region. I would need a costume to represent the District of Columbia.

I loved cherry blossoms and wanted to create a costume to showcase these beautiful flowers which were given as a gift to the United States from Japan in 1912. This was the same year the Girl Scouts were founded and was an amazing coincidence because this was my platform for my reign.

My nail technician and Philippine beauty, Emerly Drye, of fifteen years had a client who was a designer and referred me to her. The designer was specifically a wedding gown designer, named Irina Ciabonu. She was originally from Moldova, near the border of Ukraine. This country is always used in princess movies, and I was beginning to believe I was in a real-life fairy tale.

I contacted her immediately to ask about making a cherry blossom costume for the Mrs. America Stage. Magically, she loved cherry blossoms and had already created the most magnificent cherry blossom wedding gown. I made an appointment and went to her boutique to try on this glorious dress.

When I arrived at her house, it looked like a castle. Getting out of my limo, actually my minivan, I walked around the house following the path to the shop located in her basement. When I knocked on the door, I was greeted by the designer. She was wearing a lace dress with pearls. She had the fairest skin and reminded me of the fairest of them all, Snow White.

When I walked into the wedding gown boutique, I immediately felt the presence of God. This was another ordained moment from above. In this room were hundreds of wedding gowns, veils, and crowns.

In this lovely room, I thought back to my Granny who was an amazing seamstress. If you remember she had made my silk costume for Miss Mingo County when I did the dance routine to "Eye of the Tiger." This time my costume would be a silk dress.

When I looked in the corner of the room, I saw the most feminine and delicate cherry blossom wedding gown. The designer said it was a size two and wasn't sure if it would fit my frame. I am a size four. But when I tried on this dress, it fit like Cinderella's slipper. At that moment, I felt like Irina was my fairy godmother. And then, she happily agreed to sponsor this dress as my costume to represent DC on the Mrs. America Stage.

I asked her if she could also make my onstage gown. I love everything white and sparkly. I tried on one of her new designs and felt it fit perfectly, just like the cherry blossom dress. Irina took a picture of me in this dress, and I posted it on my Facebook. Immediately, I got a text from my state director saying this was prohibited. My director stated she must approve the gown and it had to be made by a famous designer.

Interesting fact: Mrs. Virginia America 2020 had her gown custome made by Irina Ciobanu. I believe each state should have the same rules to make it a fair playing field.

I shopped at several boutiques and found an emerald, green mermaid gown with Swarovski crystals embellished on the bodice by a well-known designer. My director approved this gown. I loved it but my heart never left the beautiful white dress created by Irina, that sparkled like a diamond.

That was my first choice and I always wonder if I had worn that gown, would it have gotten me closer to winning the Mrs. America Crown.

Chapter 28

New Horizons

"For my thoughts are not your thoughts, nor your ways my ways," says the Lord. "For as the heavens are higher than the earth, so are my ways higher than your ways and my thoughts than your thoughts"

Isaiah 55:8 -9 (NIV)

I was happy to leave the rugged mountains of West Virginia and go to the rolling hills of Raleigh, North Carolina.

At the age of twenty-seven, I had experienced so much heartache and disappointment in trying to find true love and the perfect career, but good things were finally on the horizon.

When I got to Raleigh, I had four weeks of intensive training. The good news is my younger sister also got hired with Midway Airlines so we would go through the training process together. At first, I thought training to be a flight attendant would be easy, but they called this Barbie boot camp for a reason.

Midway Airlines only had one aircraft to learn about since it was a startup company. The first week of training was learning all about the aircraft, where the emergency equipment was located and how to use it. The second week of training was learning about first aid. Some of the procedures we learned consisted of how to help a choking victim (the Heimlich Remover); how to use oxygen if someone could not breathe; how to use a splint for a broken arm or leg; how to stop profuse bleeding and even how to deliver a baby on the plane. At that time, I never thought I would have to use these procedures, but because of this training, many years later, I saved the life of my son. At the age of fifteen, my son and family were at a restaurant in a resort hotel. I realized my son was choking and screamed for help. No one was on staff to help a choking victim. I gave him the Heimlich. After the third try, the steak that got lodged in his throat finally came up and he was able to breathe again. Thank God for that training!

The third week of training was learning about customer service. We were taught how to greet the customer, take orders, how to fill out liquor forms, money collection and food preparation. We learned about first class service versus economy. And finally, we learned how to show the in-flight safety video. I felt I knew a lot about customer service after my first job as a salesperson. My duties were to call prospective students from the phone book, have them come to the college and enroll them in two-year associate programs. This job was going to be a lot easier!

The fourth week was a compilation of everything we learned in the first three weeks. We had oral drills where our trainers would have us scream our commands for emergency evacuations. At the window, if we were one of the flight attendants for this drill, we would have to start shouting commands and take out the window of the aircraft. Then we would go out of the window onto the wing. We would call the invisible passenger to come out after us. If it was land evacuation, the invisible passengers would jump from the wing. If it was a water landing, we would have to get out the raft from the overhead compartment located above the emergency window seat and activate it. Then throw it into the water so the invisible passengers could jump in the raft.

We also had a written test. Once we passed the oral and written tests, we were placed on probation for nine months. After probation, if we fulfilled all our requirements as a flight attendant, we would be a full-time employee with benefits. Up to this point in my life, this were the most intense training I had ever experienced, but it was also the most glorious time. I loved everything about being a flight attendant. I loved people, helping others, and traveling.

I got to work with my sister who I had always loved with all my heart from the moment she was born. She was four years younger than me, but people thought we were twins. She was the blonde, and I was the brunette.

This was going to be the glamorous life!

As a flight attendant, as soon as I got off performance probation, I was able to get buddy passes for my family and friends. Buddy passes were discounted tickets to fly to all the destinations that the company went throughout the US and the Caribbean.

My flight attendant sister, other siblings and I decided to pick Cancun as our first travel destination. It was going to be an exciting island adventure.

My parents were not too excited about all their kids being on the same plane at the same time. What if someone got sick? What if there was an emergency? Or in the worst-case scenario, what if there was a plane crash? The good news is we made it safely to our final destination.

Growing up, my parents would take us to Myrtle Beach, South Carolina, for summer vacation. We would go with our cousins, grandparents, aunts, and uncles. It was a beautiful beach. The color of the ocean was dark blue. This is where most West Virginia families went on their summer vacation.

As we were getting ready to land in Cancun, I looked out the window and the color of this ocean was the most beautiful turquoise blue. Paradise found. This island looked majestic and walking off the airplane, hearing the band play Caribbean Tunes made me feel like a Caribbean Queen.

Chapter 29

Bath Robe to Royal Robes

"Do not come any closer, "God said. "Take off your sandals, for the place where you are standing is holy ground"

Exodus 3:50 (NIV)

Two years ago, on a Sunday evening, I would have been in my bathrobe taking care of the kids. But tonight, I was going down the escalator in the loveliest Designer Gown. I was wearing a gown created by an Egyptian Designer based in the DMV. The lovely gown was embellished with pink petals. It was feminine and exquisite just like the Salamander Hotel in Washington DC.

This event was called The Gatsby Showcase, a fashion show to promote African American Designers in DC and raise money for minority startup entrepreneurs. I was invited to be a guest as Mrs. DC America 2020. Vivica Fox, well known Hollywood Actress was the presenter of the night, and the showstopper was supermodel Beverly Johnson. She was the first African American woman to grace the covers of many iconic magazines.

Before winning the crown, I was a housewife in the suburbs, but now I was part of the social scene in Washington DC. I attended the event with my model friend and co-host/singer of Singles in the City – DC. In attendance were models, beauty queens, designers, and actors.

Two months before I had produced Singles in the City – DC. I had never gone to school for production but felt God had put it on my heart to produce this show. God truly wanted me to bring Godliness and wholesomeness back to the District of Columbia. I produced a dating show like the "Dating Game "from the 70's. I wrote the production, found sponsors, picked the perfect bachelor and bachelorette, picked the contestants, and wrote the script. We sold seventy-five seats, which was the maximum for the venue. This was my second production, and it was a great success.

Tonight, the venue was much bigger. Five hundred people were in attendance. This was a yearly event. Two different designers were showcasing their designs on the runway. The first designer was Anya by Vivien. She had long gowns that were breathtaking and short cocktail dresses with ruffles. One long gold gown caught my eye and was reminiscent of Hollywood Glamour. The next designer was Miguel Wilson Collection. He was a designer for men. He had unique suits including a red sequin suit that would be perfect for a Christmas or holiday party.

After the fashion show was a fundraiser to help promote minority entrepreneurs. The one lady was from Africa and had grown up never owning a pair of shoes. She was now the owner of a footwear company. This reminded me of my Papaw Tom who also grew up in poverty and went to school with no shoes and holes in his pants. He was so embarrassed that he quit school at the age of fifteen and went to work in the coal mines.

That was a pivotal moment for my grandfather. It changed his destiny. I believed my destiny was also getting ready to change. I had just been invited by a Pakistani Designer to choreograph and walk in New York Fashion Week for February 2023. As I walked out of this venue, looking up at the chandelier, I thought how God's light had shined on my life. He had taken me from a bath robe to royal robes. What is your dream? Even when it seems too late, God is still working. And even though my reign was over, I felt like this was just the beginning of the crown.

Chapter 30

Be Okay with You

*"Therefore, I tell you, do not worry about your life,
what you will eat or drink; or about your body, what you will wear.
Is not life more than food, and the body more than clothes"*

Matthew 6:25 (NIV)

I remember at the age of thirteen, my sister Wendy was fourteen, she had the most glorious long hair. It was so thick and long that she should have been in a shampoo commercial! My hair was short and thinner. I permed it every three months to give it volume. Also, the 80's style was curled and teased. It was the era of Madonna. I prayed every day for my hair to grow but to no avail, it stayed the same length, above my shoulders. The good news is even though I had short, permed hair, I was still able to win the coveted crowns of Miss Magnolia Fair and Miss Mingo County. I learned through these experiences that the length of your hair does not define beauty.

After college, times changed, and straight hair was in vogue. This was the era of Christy Brinkley, Pamela Anderson, Farrah Fawcett, and Cheryl Tiegs. All these supermodels were blonde. I was brunette. I felt like I needed to be blonde to be pretty. I dyed my hair blonde for seven fanatical years. Looking back, I realize it took away my natural beauty. Some people are born to be blonde, but I finally realized I was born to be brunette.

Then, fast forward to being a flight attendant. On the six-year anniversary of working for the airline, there was a big pay raise. The joke was either a boob job or BMW. Unfortunately, at the six-year mark, the tragedy of September 11th happened, and the airline almost went bankrupt. I really had wanted that BMW. I am still waiting for my dream car. As far as the boob job, I already had big boobs and a push up bra did wonders.

Another fun fashion faux pas was in the 90's. It was very in style to have thin eyebrows. I had never plucked my eyebrows. My hair was not thick, but my eyebrows were the perfect thickness. Then my sister and I decided to follow the fashion trend and we plucked our eyebrows like the Spice Girls, the super popular girl band from the UK. After doing this, we realized we looked like aliens. It took away our beauty, so we anxiously waited for our eyebrows to grow back. We were very lucky because a lot of women followed this trend, and their eyebrows never grew back. What I learned is eyebrows really define the eyes and add beauty to the face.

Then at the age of fifty-four, even though I still had very few wrinkles, I felt pressure to get Botox. Even girls in their twenties were getting this procedure. I was referred to a spa and got this procedure under my eyes where I have smile lines. At first, I felt fine, and the lines disappeared and made me look refreshed. Then an hour after leaving the spa, I had a horrible pain in the back of my neck. It felt like someone had hit me. The pain went away after a couple days, and I looked a little younger, so I was happy with the results. I then went back three months later after the Botox had dissolved and tried it again. I had the same reaction. Shortly after this, I met a lady who had a stroke from getting these injections. I decided I would rather have a couple wrinkles and be in perfect health.

When I won the crown of Mrs. DC America 2020 at the age of fifty-five, I received a skin care package from Nova Derm Institute. Afsheen Ather, owner, and skin care specialist of this medical facility that did laser treatments. This is a holistic approach and truly turned back time. I highly recommend laser treatments to diminish fine lines, lift and tighten skin in a very natural way.

After a lifetime of trying to change my appearance to look prettier from: perming my hair, changing from brunette to blonde, plucking my eyebrows, and getting Botox, just to name a few, I realized being a natural queen is the best option.

Chapter 31

The Hidden Price

"Now to him who is able to do immeasurably more than all we ask or imagine, according to his power that is at work within us"

Ephesians 3:20 (NIV)

How much does it cost to be in a pageant? It depends on the system and the director. The registration fee to be in the Mrs. DC America Pageant was moderately expensive. My husband and I had just spent thousands to find the right photographer and get the perfect modeling pictures. When I got home from the fashion show, we consulted about competing in this pageant. We decided not to at this time. I decided to focus completely on my modeling dreams.

Two months later, I got a call from the state director. She said she would like me to be in the spring fashion segment for Fox 5 and asked if I was available. I showed up the next day for the show with white pants, a yellow top and yellow high heel shoes. It was an amazing day, and I really enjoyed this second opportunity to model again.

After the show, she asked again if I would compete for Mrs. DC America 2020. She recommended recruiting sponsors. I contacted my dentist, Dr. Bunin, and my best friend Kathy Keller. They both agreed to pay half to help me compete for this prestigious title. I called the state director and signed up the next day.

The price of this pageant would be much more than expected, but winning the crown changed my life and was worth the investment. In the end, I was blessed to have sponsors who believed in me and gave me the courage to resurrect the crown.

Chapter 32

The History of Beauty Pageants

"For we are God's handiwork, created in Christ Jesus to do good works, which God prepared in advance for us to do"

Ephesians 2:10 (ESV)

The modern beauty pageants' origin is traceable to Atlantic City's Inter-City Beauty Contest in 1921. The pageant was created to entice summer tourists to stay in town past Labor Day Weekend. This is where the Miss America Pageant was born. The first Miss America was Margaret Gorman, and she was from Washington D.C. At that time, they did not have an age restriction. She was sixteen years old. Now contestants must be at least seventeen years old to compete in this pageant system. In 1923, the pageant became so popular that they had over 300,000 people flocking to the boardwalk to see the beautiful women competing from all over the country.

Atlantic City has a special place in my heart because this is where my dad met my mom. My mom was working in Atlantic City in the summer as a waitress and my dad was stationed at Cape May with the United States Coast Guard. My dad went to the restaurant where my mom was working to order a sandwich and I believe it was love at first sight. Their very first evening was watching the Miss America Pageant on the boardwalk. My dad said my mom should have been on that stage and if she had competed, she would have won the crown.

Vanessa Williams was the first African American to be crowned Miss America in 1984. She was my favorite Miss America of all time. I really respect her because even though she made youthful mistakes and lost the crown, she learned, overcame, and pursued her passion becoming a famous singer, actor, and model. She also paved the way for all women to capture the crown.

In Venezuela, and other South American countries, girls attend finishing school to learn how to walk, talk and present themselves as a crown holder. They also offer hormone therapies to slow down puberty to grow taller. Often these bootcamps encourage girls to have surgery at the age of twelve. I strongly disagree with this practice. The French also dispute this practice. Their viewpoint and law are completely opposite. Girls are not allowed to compete until the age of thirteen. They believe it is extremely destructive for their self-esteem. The Philippines sends their pageant hopefuls to training school for six months where they are taught posture, public speaking and the walk called the "Passarella" (signature walk) which is meant to leave a mark in competitions and are the fiercest competitors of the crown. They currently hold the most titles from the main pageants called the Big 4 which include: Miss World, Miss Universe, Miss International, and Miss Earth.

Chapter 33

Creating Mr. DC

"But he who is noble plans noble things, and on noble things he stands"

Isaiah 32:8 (ESV)

After returning from competing in Mrs. America, I was asked to be a host for my own show. This was not a paid job, but the opportunity presented itself, so I said yes to this new position.

My sister had been a news anchor/reporter for over twenty years at this time on the Christian Broadcasting Network. I had been watching her and learned a lot from her style of reporting. She traveled all over the world and had many exciting adventures. She had many serious stories including one where she reported near the Gaza Strip during a bombing campaign and adventurous stories where she climbed Mt. Kilimanjaro and Mt. Everest to base camp.

As a host, I would not be doing any world travels like my sister. I would be reporting from a small studio in Washington DC. The owner of this network gave me the opportunity to create my own show. I had a lot of dreams come true in 2020 so I decided to call my segment "Dream Big." My job was to interview one person per month. I posted on my Facebook to find people to interview about their dreams and I had an overwhelming response. A lot of people had big dreams and I was excited to share them with the world. This segment was a small audience, but it was a huge success.

After being with this network for several months, one of the other hosts asked if I would be interested in creating a Mr. DC Pageant. I had just returned from competing in Mrs. America and knew the power of the crown. As Mrs. DC America 2020, it had given me a platform and a voice to help others. I was very excited about this new adventure and put all my heart and soul into this new project.

There are hundreds of pageants for women but very few pageants/competitions for men. My vision was to crown an honorable man that was committed to his family, the community, and his profession. We decided to call the pageant Mr. DC. I had never done a production or even gone to school for this type of work, but I had won three crowns in my lifetime and used these experiences to create my production.

The first task at hand was to get sponsors. The cost of the venue was $3,000.00 which was very cheap for MGM, but it was 2021 and Covid was still causing fear.

A lot of places were still closed, and many businesses were going bankrupt. This world-renowned venue was happy to rent to us for such an amazing event. I worked tirelessly for three months to get my incredible sponsors. Some of these sponsors were personal friends and local businesses that supported me during my reign.

Once I raised the money, the network and I were supposed to sign a contract for the venue. The organization pulled out at the last minute, and I was expected to sign the contract. At that moment, I wanted to quit, but then I realized I was a winner. Winners do not quit. I had quit so many times and I would not ever quit again. Whatever it took, I would finish this project. I was in tears over this because I trusted this company to be committed like me. I already recruited the twelve men competing and had a passion to uplift men in the community. My husband agreed that we would sign the contract. We did not have event insurance, so I called my brother he helped us to purchase the right coverage.

Thinking back to my contract with Mrs. DC America, I wish I had learned my lesson. Without a legal contract, I realized I was completely on my own.

As a team, I had five other hosts who were helping plan the event. We would meet once a week on zoom and go over all the details. I was very serious about this pageant/competition because I wanted to honor men like my husband who had extraordinary accomplishments, were committed to their families and their professional careers.

After I got the sponsors, I wrote the production. I used all my previous pageant experience, including what I learned during my week at Mrs. America, to make this an incredible show. One of the hosts on the team had a nonprofit so we agreed to have the money directly deposited into that account. Once again, I did not have any contract and that was my biggest regret.

I did not realize we would sell every seat that night. We sold two hundred and fifty seats. The judging was based on: Walk in suit, personality, talent, and onstage question. Every guy in the competition came on the stage and fought for the crown. All the men were winners in my eyes.

My parents came all the way from West Virginia to see my production, both my sisters Nancy and Wendy, my niece, my husband, and kids were in the audience. I had chosen a yellow sequin dress that sparkled like the sun. I was supposed to be one of the hosts, but the team thought I should help behind the scenes. Looking back, why did I allow this? This was my show, and I was supposed to be the host of the show. I wrote, produced, got all the talent, raised all the money, and signed the contract for the venue. Note to self: Sometimes you just have to laugh and adjust your crown.

After the show, I immediately parted ways with this organization. All money from the sponsors and ticket sales were deposited into their nonprofit account. I had done most of the work and got no credit. This was a charity gala. The charity never received any money, I was never reimbursed for all my expenses and my sponsors never got their Mr. DC Calendars. This made me think back to the story my dad cautioned us about, his friend getting fired for being dishonest.

I learned so much from writing this production. I had failed so many times in my life but what I had learned from this pageant was priceless. I did not have millionaires backing this event. I paid for the venue with my amazing sponsors and other outstanding expenses were paid with ticket revenue.

I had created my own production with the passion I had for the crown.

Chapter 34

---∞---

Au Natural

"I praise you, for I am fearfully and wonderfully made; marvelous are your works; and that my soul knows well"

Psalms 139:14 (NKJV)

I read somewhere a long time ago that you can tell the story of a person's life on their face when they are older. I never understood that until I turned fifty.

For this special event, I planned to celebrate my birthday in Las Vegas. This is where I got engaged and was one of my favorite destinations on the planet. This dessert town had incredible fashion, spas, pools, restaurants, and entertainment.

Even though I had just turned a half a century old, I felt young. Usually, women at the age of fifty have grown kids but because I got married later in life, my daughter was seven and my son was nine. By societal standards I was considered middle aged, but I had very few wrinkles and was still bikini ready.

For my birthday, I had invited my mom, sisters, cousins, best friends Kathy Keller and Laura Wissing and Aunt Tish to this celebration. On our first night, we decided to go to the rooftop bar at our hotel that overlooked the city. My mom gave a pep talk to our group and said we were going to stay out all night and celebrate because we could sleep when we were dead. My mom had gotten married in her early twenties and I felt like tonight she was celebrating all her missed birthday celebrations. My aunt who was only a year older than me and a blonde bombshell had given me a headband to wear that said "Birthday Girl" on it. Walking into the bar I felt like a celebrity. All eyes were on me and my crowd. The DJ was playing the song. "Can't Feel My Face" by The Weeknd. I am not sure about the lyrics, but it had a great beat. Girls and guys were dancing everyone and dressed for many occasions.

As soon as I got to the bar to buy a drink with my posse, a group of guys from Las Vegas were behind us. They were there for a bachelor party. They came up to me and wished me happy birthday. Then they told me I was such a natural beauty. I was from West Virginia and thought everyone was "au natural" but what I learned that night was Las Vegas had a different type of beauty.

Wearing my birthday crown, I thought to myself, *this is a Kim Kardashian world!*

Chapter 35

Heartbreak in Pittsburgh

"Above all else, guard your heart, for everything you do flows from it"

Proverbs 4:23 (NIV)

After living in Raleigh, North Carolina for two years, I was ready to set my sights on a major airline. My sister Nancy and I decided to apply for US Airways. The company had hubs all over the country, and we decided to pick Pittsburgh as our first choice. This was on the East Coast and only three hours from our home, Almost Heaven, West Virginia.

We sent our applications in and waited anxiously for a reply. It was very competitive getting hired for a major airline but now that we had two years of flight attendant experience, we would have a better chance of getting hired. After three weeks, we got a letter stating we were both accepted for training. This was super exciting because we had traveled very little, and this would give us the opportunity to travel all over the world.

The song "Breakin Up is Hard to Do" by Neil Sedaka should have been my theme song. I had found love again but not for long. We had been dating for six months. Once again, I believed this handsome guy was Mr. Right. This unexpected romance happened when my sister Nancy and I went to a popular dance club in town and danced the night away. All my heartache from my last relationship seemed to be fading away. At that moment someone bumped into me. I turned around and this guy that looked like John F. Kennedy Jr. smiled at me. This time I was not going to fall so fast. I did not want another dangerous liaison. Then the lights came on and the guy asked for my number. He was wearing a white T-shirt, so I took a pen from my purse and wrote my number on his shirt. Cell phones were not invented yet, but we had a Kodak camera and were taking pictures all night long. The next day I got the photos developed and put the picture of my mystery guy in my photo album. Then I waited for him to call. Three months had gone by, and I had not heard from him. Maybe it was not meant to be.

Since I was still single and carefree, my sister and I decided to go see a popular band, *Hootie and the Blowfish* that was performing at an outdoor venue. We were in the crowd singing along with the band and then I saw the mystery guy in the crowd. Suddenly he was staring at me and with a big smile on his face, came over and said "Hello." He said he was sorry he had not called me. He had accidentally washed the white t shirt and tried to decipher the numbers, but it was impossible. He told me his name was Jay and that he worked for FedEx. He asked me for my number, and we set a rendezvous to go to dinner. The amazing part of this story is he was from Pittsburgh. Maybe this was destiny after all.

Once I moved to Pittsburgh, he planned to relocate back to his hometown. But as time went by, he decided to stay in Raleigh. He was meeting other pretty girls. He told me he wanted a career girl that was financially secure.

I was twenty-nine years old. My heart was broken again. I thought this guy really loved me and wanted a future. We had been dating for a year. I had met his parents on several occasions and felt such a bond with his mother. She was Italian and her chef specialties were homemade French toast and gnocchi. She would have been the perfect mother-in-law. But just like the theme song from Titanic, "My heart Will Go On".

I was still old-fashioned and was going to wait for my prince. I loved being a flight attendant and even though I did not make a lot of money, I got to travel the whole world for free. I personally felt like a millionaire.

I had so much heartache. As soon as we broke up, I decided to move to Washington DC. US Airways had a hub and my other sister Wendy had just moved to this international city. This was the heartbeat of the world. If I had seen the future, I would not have believed it. God says, "Seek ye first the Kingdom of God and all these things will be given." I had been seeking God and His plan for many years but love and marriage were nowhere in sight. God works in mysterious ways. I had to be heart broken or I would have never moved to DC.

My husband and the crown were waiting for me.

Chapter 36

My Pageant Playbook

"Do you see a man skilled in his work?
He will stand before kings;
he will not stand before obscure men"

Proverbs 22:29 (ESV)

Pageants are divided into local, state, national, international, and global systems.

Mrs. DC America was a State Pageant.

The first play is to find out about the pageant system you are competing in. There are hundreds of systems with different requirements. The Mrs. America System focuses on highlighting married women who are devoted to their family, their community and profession. They also require a platform that is community driven. The platform I chose as you know was the Girl Scouts because this organization was very close to my heart. I was a Girl Scout, and my daughter was a Girl Scout.

The second play is to hire a pageant coach that has been a winner in this system. This is very important because this coach will know what type of questions the judges will ask, the style of onstage dress to purchase, what type of queen they want to represent their state or district and how to capture the crown. My pageant coach was Marta Bota and I highly recommend her for this system.

The third play is to hire a walking coach who has been a winner in this system on the state level. The walk-in pageantry is very important because it shows confidence. To be the queen, you must have confidence. The art of the walk is different for every pageant system.

The fourth play is to hire a trainer. The fitter your body is, the better you will look in your gown, interview attire, bathing suit and onstage costume. Working out also reverses age. Other benefits include being healthier and looking younger.

The fifth play is to get the perfect dress. I recommend finding a local designer to create your dream gown. If you cannot find a local designer, I recommend Sheri Hill or New York Designer Marc Defang. Both are American designers who specialize in the most feminine and luxurious pageant gowns.

The sixth play is to hire the perfect hair and makeup team. I believe you should do a trial with several different hair and makeup specialists to find the perfect fit for you. Finding a team that brings out your natural beauty is the best team.

If you play by the rules, you can win the crown.

Chapter 37

Competing for Mrs. America

*"Who satisfies your desires with good things
so that your youth is renewed like the eagle's"*

Psalms 103:5 (NIV)

After competing and winning the crown of Mrs. DC America 2020, another bigger dream from long ago was getting ready to happen. I was going to compete for Mrs. America at the age of fifty-five.

David and Elaine Marmel created the Mrs. America Pageant in 1971 to highlight married women that were devoted to family, their profession, and the community. As soon as I realized I would be competing for the national title, I hired my state coach to prepare me for the interview. I also hired a former Mrs. DC America who had competed twice on the national stage to help with my walk. I loved this system because to me it represented conservative and wholesome values. On my birthday, six months prior to the pageant, David Marmel died. I was praying the ownership would remain in the hands of Elaine Marmel. It was very upsetting to the entire Miss/Mrs. America Family, but his wife continued the pageant with the help of owners/sponsors of the Westgate Hotel.

The schedule was set for the pageant and all the contestants arrived a day before the pageant or the day of check in. I arrived a day early thinking I would have time to be well rested. Unfortunately, everyone came the day before, so I did not check in to my room until midnight. I really was hoping to get my beauty sleep.

The next morning was a whirlwind of going to makeup and hair, picking up dance costume and bathing suit. Then we met in the lobby for a group picture in the evening. I did not realize that this was the beginning of the judging process. I wore a white dress with an elegant bow and silver sequin high heels. All the ladies were dressed to impress. It was so wonderful to dress up. Throughout my life, I have had endless experiences where I was told I was too overdressed. I believe we must dress for success. When we dress the part, we get the part.

The next five days were rehearsals for the big production. We would learn the choreography for the dance routine and when each contestant would walk on stage for gown, costume, and bathing suit. I had hired a hair and makeup team for each day. I also had a dress for every rehearsal and felt prepared and ready to compete for this iconic crown.

When I showed up at rehearsal on the first day, everyone was dressed hair and makeup ready like me. Even though I was fifty-five, I still felt I had a chance to capture the crown. I did not think I was the fairest of them all. I was thirty-three years older than the youngest contestant. But I was told I had a timeless beauty and with my young daughter by my side, I would continue to promote my platform of mentoring young girls to become future leaders through the Girl Scouts of the United States of America.

But as soon as rehearsal began, I saw that most girls had amazing walks. I had focused on preparing for the interview, costume, and onstage gown. I had a nice walk, but these walks showed me why supermodels such as Christy Turlington and Naomi Campbell get paid millions.

I realized I was not prepared for the National Stage, but I would give a million percent. My husband, precious son and daughter, brother-in-law, parents, newlywed sister Wendy and husband Bill, my devoted friends Kevin and Rebecca Harris and Don and Laura Wissing came to cheer me on.

The Westgate Hotel had previously been called the International Hotel. This was also referred to as Elvis Presley's home. The amazing part of this story is in 1969, my parents went to see Elvis perform on this same stage. I was four years old at the time. My parents never imagined in their wildest dreams their daughter would be competing at the age of fifty-five for the crown of Mrs. America.

The sponsors for the Mrs. America Pageant were the owners of the Westgate Hotel and the winner would be promoting their platform for 2020. Their beautiful daughter had died of a drug overdose, and their focus was picking a queen who could promote that cause. I thought mentoring young girls was the perfect fit because when you promote leadership and confidence, you are less likely to give in to peer pressure. One of the top five contenders had recovered from an addiction to drugs. But I must say, thankfully, love was my only addiction.

The day of Mrs. America had arrived. I would walk on that stage, first and foremost for my beloved daughter. I wanted to show her and all women that you must be bold and pursue your dreams. Even if society labels you "past your prime," I was going to show the world, it is never too late. I also wanted to inspire my son to show him that he can accomplish anything in life with a goal, hard work, and persistence. The first part of the production was fitness. I loved our bathing suit selection which was a beautiful pink one piece. I felt I was in the best shape of my life at the age of fifty-five. During my reign, as previously mentioned, I was sponsored by Fitness Together in Georgetown, owner, Stacy Dykman.

The second part of the production was a dance number. During the gown presentation, I emerged wearing my emerald, green dress. Because it was a married pageant; we had our husbands escort us when we went out to announce our state title. I was told my whole life," It can't be done," but my vision was not giving up, it was climbing the mountain. So, from the depths of despair to this national stage victory prevailed. There was no doubt that God had prepared me for this moment. And my husband was definitely a love worth waiting for and the reason I was able to compete on this iconic stage.

Another favorite moment in the show was the costumes. If you recall, my designer Irina Ciabonu had made a custom cherry blossom wedding gown that I wore to represent Washington DC. I had a beautiful parasol to match the dress. In 1912, the Japanese had given Cherry Blossoms to the United States as a gift after the war. This was the same year the Girl Scouts was founded, which was my platform for my reign.

When they called the top fifteen, my name was not called. It brought me back to the Junior Miss Pageant. My mom was in the audience but this time I believe she was proud of me. Only fifty-one women in the United States get chosen once a year to compete in this pageant. I had learned so much in this week and I would take what I had learned to make my life extraordinary. Even though I had not won this National Crown, the Mrs. America Pageant had changed my life.

Chapter 38

Helping Others

"And do not forget to do good and to share with others, for with such sacrifices God is pleased"

Hebrews 13:16 (NIV)

With my platform, as soon as I was crowned Mrs. DC America 2020, I also became the leader of my daughter's troop. One of the requirements for my reign was to have four appearances a month.

During this time everything was closed due to covid. This was a fabulous time to do appearances with my Girl Scouts. I would have a meeting once a week to comply with my contract for my reign.

I had been a Girl Scout as a little girl and this platform was very close to my heart. I did not realize as a leader the adversities I would encounter with the other leader of this troop. This specific troop was multi-level. I took my leadership course online and then replaced the lady who was resigning from my position. I was happy to be a team player. I knew that the senior level Girl Scout mom oversaw finances. Her daughter was inactive. As the middle school leader with twelve Girl Scouts, I wanted to have access to the bank account because we had money from the previous year from cookie sales. This money was supposed to be used for Girl Scout activities. Unfortunately, the year of my reign, it seemed like I could never get money from the Girl Scout account. You would have thought I was Sandra Bullock in the movie *Oceans 8* planning a heist, but I just wanted the money my Girl Scouts had earned from the previous year. My amazing brother-in-law, Greg Roberts, who owns a plumbing company sponsored my troop for $1,000.00 including my Girl Scout parents who also donated to make this troop one of the best in the country.

The first lesson plan I created was making face masks. At that time there was a shortage of face masks at hospitals. I was from a different generation. My grandmother had taught me to sew, and I also signed up to take sewing in home economics in high school. To complete the class, we were required to design and sew our own outfit and then wear it to school. I loved sewing and felt like it was a lost art. I had taught my daughter to sew, and she had her own sewing machine. The other girls in the troop were novices. They were amazing students and they enjoyed learning the basics. We ended up making around a hundred fashion masks for hospitals.

Another lesson I created was to make kindness rocks. Everyone was very afraid of Covid and what was going to happen. My Girl Scouts wrote uplifting words on rocks and painted them. Then we delivered the rocks and placed them in mailboxes around the community. The beautiful part of this story is that Ashburn has a community Facebook group, and someone wrote on the public page how thankful they were for receiving this kindness rock in such a lonely and uncertain time. As a leader, even though we did not have a million dollars, we were making a difference in the community and beyond.

I also had the girls learn CPR so if they ever needed to help the community, they would be prepared. We hired Mary Beth Pratt, owner of Mission4life accredited BSN, RN, CPR and first aid instructor to teach the girls how to learn this life saving technique.

Then they all received a certificate of completion through the American Heart Association.

My Girl Scouts loved animals, so we made homemade treats for dogs and cats. Then we delivered them to different rescues in the area. We really wanted to pet the animals but because of covid, we were only able to drop off the treats at the front desk. Then we celebrated "kindness to pets' day" and had everyone bring their dog or cat to the meeting. Everyone had dogs so we took the dogs for a long walk around the neighborhood. It was a sight to see with twelve teenage girls walking their adorable pups.

My girls were more interested in the arts than in camping. One of our most exciting activities was going to New York. I had two other moms volunteer to help drive and we bought tickets to see *Aladdin* and went to New York City for the day. I wanted my Girl Scouts to see through this musical that dreams can come true.

During my time as a leader of the troop, the Girl Scouts of America publicly denounced Amy Coney Barrett Supreme Court Justice as a Girl Scout for being pro-life. I am pro-life and was shocked by this organization that was founded by Juliet Gordan Lowe who was known to be a devout Christian. The Girl Scouts are still a nondenominational Christian organization welcoming girls of all faiths.

I was also discriminated against because I had conservative values. I have traveled all over the world and have friends from all political parties, ethnicities, and religions. As a leader, I was required to appoint an assistant leader. I chose my makeup artist and one of my best friends Mervat who was originally from Jordan. Her daughter was also thirteen. She was not only an amazing assistant leader, but she was also a great defender of my character.

By the ending of my reign, my Girl Scouts and I had performed hundreds of hours of kindness acts and received a medal from the

President of the United States for outstanding service in 2020. As the queen, it was truly an honor to be a leader and help others.

Chapter 39

The Judge

*"The integrity of the upright guides them,
but the unfaithful are destroyed by their duplicity"*

Proverbs 11:3 (NIV)

To be asked to be a judge is a great honor. I have always been on the other side as the contestant. But after winning the crown of Mrs. DC America 2020 and competing at Mrs. America on the National Stage in 2021, I was contacted by the Miss/Ms./Mrs. Pakistan Organization. This international pageant was held at the MGM near the National Harbor.

Walking into this venue, I was greeted by the owner of this pageant system. His name is Ali. For this upscale event, he was dressed in a tuxedo, and I was wearing a blue chiffon dress designed by Portia and Scarlett. Wearing this dress, I felt like the queen and was ready to judge the contestants with a pure heart. I was one of nine judges on this magical night. The other judges were all of Pakistani descent. These men and women were from all different professions and age groups. The one judge who sat right beside me was a Pakistani Fashion Designer specializing in bridal. As the pageant was about to begin, we were all handed binders with all the contestants' names and bios. I was seated in the middle of all the judges, center stage.

The judges were instructed to tally the scores by beauty, talent, and onstage questions. All the contestants had something special but the highest score for each category would determine the winners. One of the talents that stood out was in the Miss division. The nineteen-year-old beauty painted a picture with classical music playing in the background. She had five minutes to paint this artwork. When she turned it around to the audience, it was a beautiful portrait of her mother who was in the audience. The other talent that was informative and entertaining was from another contestant in the Miss division who showed the audience how to do CPR on a dummy to the background music of "Stayin Alive" from the soundtrack *Saturday Night Fever.*

What I learned from judging is that beauty is the number one factor, but the winner must also have stage presence, a beautiful smile, sweet spirit, and a graceful walk. In the end, it is a feeling called the "It" factor. As a Christian, I would call it the anointing.

The most heartfelt part of this pageant was that it was dedicated to the founder who had also been a pageant queen. She had died in a tragic car wreck thirteen years prior to this event. The brother of the founder, Ali, decided to produce the pageant again to continue her legacy of uplifting outstanding women in the Pakistani Community. As he was standing on the stage, I wondered how I had been chosen to be one of the judges from all the other beauty queens, designers, and leaders in the DMV. Then Ali told the story of his sister and the day of the car crash. It was December 1st. This was the same day my daughter was born thirteen years before. I believe this was a heavenly sign that his sister in heaven had chosen me to be one of the judges. This was a crowning moment from above.

Chapter 40

Singles in the City - DC

"And above all this put-on love, which binds everything together in perfect harmony"

Colossians 3:14 (ESV)

After creating Mr. DC 2021, even though the production did not turn out as planned, I realized I had an incredible gift and God wanted me to use it for his glory. God had placed it on my heart to write a production to bring love and marriage back to the Nation's Capital. Being Mrs. DC America 2020, I wanted to connect the crown to the show. I chose a venue in DC called "The Crown and the Crow." The crown had given me a lot of opportunities to make a difference and I would use the profit from this production to help American Veterans and Human Trafficking Victims.

I loved the *Dating Game* from the 70's, the *Bachelor/Bachelorette* and *Dancing with the Stars*. I decided to combine all these shows into one production. I chose my model friend Debra Ovall to be the assistant producer, singer, and cohost of the show. I started looking for the bachelor and bachelorette. I would choose 3 contestants for each. I would also showcase a local designer, bridal designer and a jewelry designer for the show. I would include the reigning Mrs. DC America from the Mrs. America System to talk about her love story. I also added a Romantic Tae Kwon Do Routine with Mrs. Maryland 2021 and her husband who would perform this onstage in front of a live audience.

To make this show happen, I needed sponsors. I had gotten twenty-nine sponsors for my Mr. DC 2021 Pageant but because the other organization I had paired with did not fulfill the commitment to the sponsors, I would have a harder time finding these integral people to help fund this production. God was about to make miracles happen. I ended up getting five local businesses to sponsor me. They still believed in me and were willing to give me another chance. I was able to raise $1500.00. Usually, a production cost around $10,000.00 plus but I was going to trust God to meet me the rest of the way. I booked The Crown and the Crow located in the heart of DC. The cost of this venue was $3,300.00. I was able to pay a deposit of $500.00 to reserve this for the show.

I now needed a film crew because I wanted to submit this to the networks. This was another *Field of Dreams Project*. My first production was to highlight honorable men in the DMV that were devoted to family, the community, and their profession. This production was written to bring love and marriage to the Nation's Capital. I was working for God and His Kingdom. I was one week out from the live show. The weekend before I went to New York Fashion Week. I roomed with several models including Miss for Maryland America 2023. Her boyfriend had come to surprise her to see her on the runway. His name is Matias which means "Gift of God." The name of his production is Rich Creatives, and he owned a production company. I told him about my production, and he was onboard to film this for a small fee.

God had sent me another gift to showcase the power of love and the crown.

Chapter 41

Walk By Faith

"How blessed is the man who does not walk in the counsel of the wicked, Nor stand in the path of sinners, Nor sit in the seat of scoffers"

Psalms 1:1 (NASB)

Once I got back from the Mrs. America Pageant, I wanted to master the walk. I was fascinated with the walk because I realized there was magic in it. The top fifteen at Mrs. America in 2020 had million-dollar walks. I believe some contestants like my roommate Mrs. Delaware America 2020, Musulin Toomer who was also a gifted dancer was just born with this walk but most of contestants had been training for this stage and the walk since childhood.

On the first day of rehearsal, I realized I had not been prepared for this moment. Each week for 2 months prior to the competition, we would meet weekly on Zoom and go over our walk. There was no formal training, and it was not adequate for the competition I was about to compete in. These women were the best of the best. I met many contestants who had walking instructors and had been preparing and were ready for the national stage. I propose they produce a handbook at the national level that provides state directors and their contestants with a list of professional walking instructors plus interview coaches, and hair and makeup experts for each state. This would make the competition a fairer playing field.

At Mrs. America, instead of rising to the challenge, I became intimidated and insecure. Thinking to myself, *if I ever have this opportunity again, I will hire coaches who were winners on this national stage.* I had not only disappointed myself, but I felt like I had disappointed hundreds of people who were cheering me on in Washington DC and my home state of West Virginia.

When I returned home, I hired a walking coach that walked on the prestigious stage at New York Fashion Week every year. I was going to prepare for the future and walk by faith.

Then I had another opportunity to apply with Dash Talents for September 2022, a modeling agency outside of DC that was connected with VIP Pageantry. They were an organization that selected pageant queens to walk on the prestigious New York Runway. To prepare for this casting, models were asked to send a headshot, full body, resume and walking video. I was chosen to walk for an exquisite designer based in DC.

Two hundred models from DC were selected to go with Dash Talents to New York in September of 2022. I was so excited to go with my best model friend Debra Ovall and co producer of "Singles in the City." When I arrived in New York, all the models checked in to the Lavish Marriott Marquis. We would then have a schedule to get our badges, fittings, and rehearsal. "Fittings" are where the designer will select the dresses that each model will wear on the runway. I was selected to try on this black sparkly Cinderella dress. It fit me perfectly. After all the models tried on their dresses, I was told I would be walking in the Charity Gala instead of on the Runway. At first, I was disappointed but then I realized what an honor this was to wear the charity gown. I was then asked to try on a light pink dress with an elegant lace bodice. It was gorgeous and even more beautiful than the first black sparkly one.

The Charity Gala was the last event of New York Fashion Week. There were over three hundred people in the audience. Mrs. America 2022 was one of the models for this event also. After Mrs. America was introduced on stage, the DC designer was next. I walked out in that gorgeous gown. The dress sold in the thousands for an incredible cause. I believed at that moment; I was walking into my destiny.

Chapter 42

Still Standing

"I know you can do all things; no purpose of yours can be thwarted."

Job 42:2 (NIV)

Coming back from Mrs. America with no crown and not even placing in the top fifteen was heart breaking. I had devoted countless hours to my platform and had raised thousands for a charity close to my heart, the Make a Wish Foundation and the Mrs. America Platform to prevent drug addiction.

I remember my parents sitting in the audience at this grand event. I wanted to make my parents proud of me. At the age of eighty and eight-three, my parents, Kelly and Georgia, were waiting to hear the top fifteen. When my name was not called, emotions overtook my father. He walked out of the venue. He had seen all my struggles of endless heartbreak, finally finding true love and finding a successful career. He knew the blood, sweat, and tears it took for me to get to this moment from my childhood to now. My parents knew it was a long shot for me to win this title because I was one of the oldest contestants, and I was competing against fifty of the most beautiful women in the country for the Mrs. America Crown. But they believed in me and were excited to hear my name called for the top fifteen. I was not deemed a top contender for the crown at this time.

The next day, stepping on the plane in Las Vegas, unfortunately I didn't hit the jackpot this time, but I had come too far to give up. I was willing to gamble on my future plans and continue to pursue my passion to pursue my modeling dreams.

Landing at Reagan International, I stepped off the plane, still reigning as Mrs. DC America 2020. I thought if I had won Mrs. America, I would have had media to greet me at the terminal but instead I was met by the loving arms of my children, Joseph and KellyAnne.

A week later, I was invited to a party by my sponsored costume designer Irina Ciobanu. Even though I did not win, she wanted to celebrate my incredible reign. At this event, I met a makeup artist who owned Makeup and Hair by Alina Karaman and her photographer partner who owned Tanira Dove Photography. They asked if I would like to have complimentary pictures taken in my onstage gown. God truly works in mysterious ways. I was happy to collaborate with these two talented Ukrainian beauties. They asked where I would like to meet, and I chose the National Cathedral in Washington DC. These pictures were truly anointed from the heavenly realm and were some of the most beautiful of my entire reign.

Chapter 43

The Dentist and the Crown

"For the eyes of the Lord move to and fro throughout the earth that he may strongly support those whose heart is completely his"

2 Chronicles 16:9 (NASB)

I was about to meet the dentist who would help bring my buried dream back to life. Throughout the years I have had a lot of bad experiences with dentists and men.

Once again, heartbreak was on the horizon. As soon as I transferred to Marshall University, I met a guy named Gene Ray at a college bar. He was blonde, blue eyes and had a great smile. He was going to be a future dentist and his personality was magnetic. I do not believe we ever had an official date. We would meet at the bars and drink the night away. It was a three-month affair. He ended up breaking up with me. What does love have to do with it? Tina Turner and I knew all about love.

Speaking of love, I loved being a flight attendant and we had great insurance, so I made an appointment to go to the dentist for a checkup. The dentist said I had six cavities. I did not have any pain but trusted the prognosis. My mom and dad always said, "If it ain't broke, don't fix it." I got all the cavities filled but was not excited to go to the dentist again after this experience.

The next time I went to the dentist was several years later. It was the morning after my wedding. My husband and I were getting ready to go to Italy on our honeymoon. I started to have a terrible pain in my tooth. My sister-in-law who worked for a general dentist suggested I go to an endodontist. That morning, I got an emergency appointment and ended up having a partial root canal.

After this root canal, I did not go to the dentist again for many years. I do not recommend this but am just telling my dental story.

When I had another pain in my tooth, I asked my husband about his family dentist. He had been going every six months since before we were married. But his dentist was getting ready to retire. A new dentist was taking over the practice. His name was Dr. Bunin. I decided to make an appointment with him because my husband said he came highly recommended.

Back to college, the first time I met Dr. Bunin, I thought he looked like a college kid. But he had a warm smile and I thought maybe I had met my forever dentist. The whole staff at this office treated me like family. I would tell them all about my exciting moments working at the jewelry store. And my frustration about being paid eleven dollars an hour. When I quit my job and decided to pursue my real dream of being a model, the whole office cheered me on. Then when I needed sponsors to pay for my fee to enter a pageant, Dr. Bunin was the first local business to believe and invest in my dream. The moral of this story is that my dentist truly believed I deserved a crown.

Chapter 44

―――⚬∞⚬―――

The Competitors

"I praise you, for I am fearfully and wonderfully made"

Psalms 139:14 (NIV)

Standing in front of the camera in my basement for the interview segment was different than a normal pageant. This was during the pandemic, so everything was done virtually. I selected a yellow dress to wear for this interview. I rented this dress from Rent the Runway. This online store rents designer clothes for a fraction of the cost. I believe when you dress the part, you get the part. When picking the dress color, I chose yellow which represents confidence. The dress was conservative and classy. I thought about my competitors and wondered what fashion choices they selected for this crucial part of the competition. What colors did they choose, what style, what brand? Were they wearing business, cocktail or formal?

Even though this was not an in-person interview, the anticipation of giving the best answers to the questions was still overwhelming. At the same time, I was ready for this moment. If you are a football fan, I must say I prepared like the actor Mark Walberg in my favorite movie *Invincible*. This was a true story about Vince Papale who sees his wildest dreams come true when he tries out for the team and becomes a member of the Philadelphia Eagles, being the oldest rookie in NFL history. I wondered if the other five contestants had prepared at this level by hiring a pageant coach and working with a trainer.

I had prepared for this moment like the Olympics. Thirty-six years had taught me a lot about life. I had lost at the Junior Miss Pageant for the state title because I was not prepared. I would be prepared and do everything in my power to win this coveted crown. This was truly a do or die situation for me. I had studied endless hours with my heart and soul to be ready for these questions. I wondered if the other competitors studied endless hours for the interview segment.

I would not disappoint my mom again and most of all I would not disappoint myself. I believe God opened this door because I was now worthy to win this crown. The good news is I finally found true love and have been married to my husband for fifteen years. His support throughout the years helped build back my confidence. My beloved children gave me unconditional love. After all these years, I was now ready to get the touchdown and recapture the crown.

Chapter 45

Family Ties

*"Death and life are in the power of the tongue:
And they that love it shall eat the fruit thereof"*

Proverbs 18:21 (KJV)

I do not think telling your family matters is honorable. Look at Prince Harry. He recently sold his private family matters to Netflix, the tabloids and even wrote a book about his private life. What has this done for him? It has separated him from the crown. He was fifth in line for the throne. I believe we must value our family above all else.

When I won the crown of Mrs. DC America 2020, my state director decided to do a podcast on "Tragedy to Triumph." My director picked other queens in the same system to share tragic stories. I was also chosen to tell a tragic story. I had not had a perfect life but compared to these other stories my life was a fairytale.

One of the queens was a survivor of sexual abuse. Another queen who was born in the Philippines had starved as a child. Both ladies were able to overcome their circumstances and become advocates for these great causes.

Unfortunately, I was afraid to turn this assignment down because she had already threatened to take my crown once. Was I starring in the movie *Miss Congeniality*? Because my state director reminded me of Kathy Morningside!

Since I was assigned this podcast, I decided to think of how I had overcome tragedy. I had not starved as a child or overcome sexual abuse. I was very blessed in many ways. My parents have been married for over a half century! I have two brothers and two sisters and grew up with four sets of grandparents. My mom was twenty-four years old when I was born. She was still a kid compared to me having my daughter at forty-three. My mom had five kids and stayed home until we were teenagers. What I have learned from some of these tragic stories is that my mom is amazing. She protected us, made our lunches for school, and made a homemade meal every night. It was a different time when kids were seen and not heard. I never felt like my mom was my best friend, but it was a different generation. Kids were not best friends with their parents.

For the podcast, I decided to talk about "Failure is not Final". When I lost the crown at the Junior Miss Pageant, I truly felt like a failure. I did not realize at the age of eighteen that failure is not final. I wanted listeners to know that you do not have to wait thirty-six years to succeed. Failure prepares you to win. Passion, persistence, and a purpose will help you succeed. In the end, if you do not give up and keep mastering your craft, failure will prepare you to win crowns, championships and beyond.

Chapter 46

Standing On Holy Ground

"Before I formed you in the womb, I knew you; before you were born, I sanctified you; and I ordained you a prophet to the nations"

Jeremiah 1:5 (NKJV)

In the Bible, God says, "But seek ye first the kingdom of God and his righteousness and all these things will be added unto you," Mathew 6:33, KJV. After being a Girl Scout Leader during my reign and beyond, I wanted to continue to mentor young people to become future leaders.

My daughter has been attending CCD which is Catholic Education since kindergarten. After this year, she will go through a formal ceremony called "Confirmation." I volunteered to be an assistant in her classroom. This is an after-school curriculum required by the Catholic Church to learn about biblical teachings.

I have never worked at a church. When I went for my training, I remembered going to the classroom. It had a pillow in the corner that stated, "You will be amazed at the heights to which you are called." I believe God was speaking to me loud and clear.

The most important part of this two-day seminar was being told that as teachers, we were considered "boots on the ground." If a child was being abused, a teacher would be the first to see the signs. I am a part time assistant, but the full-time teachers spend more time with the children than their own parents. The speaker of this seminar told us we must alert authorities if we see any signs of child abuse. We must not remain silent. We must be a voice for the children.

As an assistant, I feel working for the church and being a teacher together is a higher calling. The book called *Chosen* is the book we have been teaching to the eighth grade classroom. Each week, we teach on a different subject related to the Bible. These young adults need to know that Divine Law cannot be changed by man, God's laws are higher than human laws. Our society has become a Godless society, but our country was founded on Christian Principals and as Christians, this is what we stand for and are called to teach to our future generations.

An example of our society turning against God's divine law is "abortion." Our Fifth Commandment in the Bible is "Thou Shall Not Kill." In some states, this is legal. Not everything that is legal is moral. My prayer in devoting my time to teaching and mentoring young people through the Church is to help them grow up to be leaders in the community and beyond. We must build the kingdom.

Chapter 47

A Blink of An Eye

"Teach us to realize the brevity of life, so that we may grow in wisdom"

Psalms 90:12 (NLT)

At fifty-seven, looking back at a lifetime with my parents, I feel so much sadness and joy. My mom was twenty-four and my dad was twenty-seven when I was born, replacing some of their own youth to raise their children.

Thinking back, I realize that my parents sacrificed everything to help us succeed. I have two brothers and two sisters. We all are college educated. How could my parents afford this on one salary? There was never a question about going to college and getting educated. It was the key to success, and we would get a degree. My mom went to college for one year and my dad graduated from Marshall University with a BA in Business Administration. My mom had different jobs throughout her life. Her most iconic position was "Deputy" to the "Sheriff," and I must admit, she was a beauty but she was tough. Her motto was, "What won't kill you will make you stronger."

Throughout my childhood and until I graduated from High School, we would go to Myrtle Beach, South Carolina every year for a summer trip and to Gatlinburg, Tennessee for our mountain get away. We did not fly but would all pile up in our station wagon for the eight hours plus drive. It was a simple life with many cherished memories.

Now my parents vacation with my husband and kids every year in the Bahamas. Instead of a station wagon, we fly Southwest. Sitting at The Cove poolside in Atlantis having tropical drinks, the Bahamian Entertainer started singing "Country Roads Take Me Home." My dad was born in South Charleston, West Virginia and my mom was born in Matewan, West Virginia. My heart will always be in West Virginia. Even in the Bahamas, we cannot escape those country roads.

Chapter 48

Fashion is not for the Faint of Heart

"Put on your new nature, created to be like God – truly righteous and holy"

Ephesians 4:24 (NLT)

Being a stay-at-home mom from my forties to fifties, I always wore Victoria Secret matching sweat outfits every day for ten years. After winning the crown, I went from sweats to ball gowns overnight! I loved dressing up and was happy to dress for success again!

As a woman in her fifties, I want to tell the elegant ladies to only wear a baseball cap when going to a National's game. After a certain age, putting on a baseball hat pulls down your face and makes you look years older. The fedora is another alternative that offers a classic, yet timeless look for women. It is perfect for almost any occasion and can be worn when going to the grocery store or attending a red-carpet event. And the floppy hat is perfect for the beach or a sunny day.

Another faux pau is wearing bright colors with big patterns. This calls attention to every flaw. If you work out, you can wear this style, but I would not throw caution to the wind otherwise.

At the beach, an ageless beauty should always wear a flowy skirt or coverup with her bikini. If ladies prefer a one-piece bathing suit, ruching which is figure flattering helps make everyone look their best. Of course, if you look like Pamela Anderson from the days of *Baywatch* I recommend buying the classic red one-piece. And if you rock the Bo Derek look from the romantic comedy *10*, you were born to wear a bikini.

When looking for comfortable shoes, I believe a heel always adds a feminine touch. From ½ to 4 inches and beyond creates elegance. My favorite high heel designer is Marc Defang. He is the leading pageant, prom, and designer footwear brand in the U.S. His shoes have a platform which creates a lift and are much more comfortable than traditional high heels. Another fashion secret is wearing nude shoes. There are nude shoes for every skin tone and this color elongates the legs. If wearing tennis shoes for other than sports, I suggest some sparkle to create a glamorous look.

If wearing workout apparel, my favorite brand is Lululemon because the cut is beautiful and youthful. My fifteen-year-old daughter and I both wear this brand. The colors and designs hide many flaws and accentuate everyone's figure. The designers behind this brand are geniuses.

Fashion is not for the faint of heart. I believe beauty favors the bold so sparkle and wear your crown.

Chapter 49

Beauty Tips from the Queen

"And who knows whether you have not come to the kingdom for such a time as this?"

Esther 4:14 (ESV)

The number one beauty tip I recommend is a smile. I always tell my kids when you smile, the world smiles with you. It makes you look more youthful because I believe happiness creates beauty. Also, when you smile gravity is turned upside down. Your face is lifted!! During my twelve-year career as a flight attendant, I smiled a lot. At the beginning of one exciting trip, I will always remember greeting this distinguished gentleman. When he walked on the plane, he looked at me with a twinkle in his eye and said, "You have a million-dollar smile." A smile is contagious and creates miles and miles of smiles. It releases dopamine which is a hormone that makes you feel happy. It also boosts your immune system so when you are healthy, you have a radiant glow.

Posture is my second beauty tip. Posture is very important as you age. Standing up straight with your shoulders back is a sign of youthfulness. As people age, they start to slump over. To keep your posture perfect, I recommend lifting weights, stability ball, Pilates, yoga, etc. I also love to dance and believe this is a beautiful way to retain your posture. When I will a little girl, I took ballet. Ballet is amazing for improving posture because every single ballet exercise uses the core. Excellent posture gives you confidence, more energy, and even helps you breathe easier. People look taller and slimmer when they stand up straight. Good posture can even make you more attractive.

Femininity is my third beauty tip. I believe a lot of women have lost this trait because to be feminine can be considered a weakness. But I believe this is a woman's beauty and superpower. Traits traditionally cited as feminine include gracefulness, gentleness, empathy, humility, and sensitivity. In western culture, pink is the color of femininity. While researching pink, it is also considered low social power and low social status whereas red is seen as powerful, dominant, and high social status. No matter what the research says, I feel prettiest in pink and that is my signature color. I love the quote, "Pink is not just a color: it's a state of mind." And never forget the crown.

JeanAnne Roberts

Chapter 50

New York Fashion Week 2023

"See then that you walk circumspectly, not as fools but as wise, redeeming the time, because the days are evil"

Ephesians 5:15 -16 (NKJV)

I had always dreamed of being a Victoria Secret Angel. Now the moment had presented itself and I was on my way to New York City to be in my first Fashion Show. New York Fashion Week was everything I imagined. As the casting director, choreographer and show opener for Randhawa Brands, I was honored to walk the runway for Amna Iman, Pakistani/Western Designer.

On February 9th, 2023, we had a caravan of eighty models from Washington D.C. to New York City for this spectacular event. Most models took trains and buses, but I drove up the East Coast in my minivan with five other fashionistas. As soon as we saw the New York Landscape, I played the song "Welcome to New York" by Taylor Swift. I love the part in the song where Taylor Swift says, "Put your broken hearts in the drawer." To get to this stage took a lot of heart break but with persistence and passion, you can achieve anything.

This brand represents young beauty, ageless beauty, curvy beauty, and people with disabilities.

We stayed at the Hilton Embassy Suite, located on Broadway. Walking into this boutique hotel, I felt a great love for this city and was excited to be chosen to walk on this prestigious stage.

The venue for this fashion show was produced by hiTechMODA and held at Gotham Hall. This historic landmark was built in 1922 featuring a 9,000 square foot ballroom with a 70-foot ceiling and an ornate skylight. It was reminiscent of an ancient amphitheater from the Roman Era.

Randhawa Brands is the designer we would be representing on this stage. This Washington D.C. designer originally from Pakistan would be showcasing her collection in three different fashion segments. Since I was the choreographer for the show, I was required to be with the models for the 11 a.m. show on February 10th. When we arrived at the venue, two hours prior there was already a line to get into the event. All models were led upstairs and put in groups to be called onto the stage at a specific time. Behind the scenes were last minute touch ups, practicing onstage walk and taking videos and pictures to post on social media.

The 10:30 a.m. show started right on time and models were lined up by designers. When Randhawa Brands was called, the Pakistani music began to play and added an elegance to the ballroom. Every model had a beautiful dress with color schemes from bridal white to dazzling red. Some of the dresses were two pieces showing a subtle sexiness and others more conservative one pieces. Each was a unique piece of art created by the designer. Two of the models I chose for this segment were Ava and Grace Krueger. They are two of the top Irish dancers in the entire world.

After this show, I went to hair and makeup to get ready for the 5 p.m. show. Each show had twenty-five models. My show had many beauty queens including my roommate from Mrs. America 2020

Musulin Toomer, Mrs. Delaware America 2020 who also came to model for this amazing brand. I also asked Lily Brasch, a beautiful model with multiple sclerosis, to walk in the show and she was an inspiration to many onstage. At the 5 p.m. show, we had a Pakistani singer, Haider Hassan. He was a dentist by day and a singer by night. He was extraordinary and truly made the stage come alive.

As the show began and the singer started singing his beautiful melody, I walked out onto the stage. I was wearing a beautiful white wedding gown. After striking a pose, I did a circle around the singer to showcase my elegant train while he serenaded me. Next, I walked to the end of the runway doing three positions to showcase the dress. At this moment, I saw cameras flashing from photographers and the crowd erupted in applause. I felt like a princess on that stage and hopefully inspired others that age does not define beauty. Many other models came out after me and the entire show was full of energy and excitement.

Many models danced to the rhythm of the beat and added extra energy to the fashion segment. The show ended with models flooding the runway. Then the designer, showstopper, and I walked center stage with one final pose, turned and all the models followed off the stage. The final curtain was the next day ending in a three-day regal affair.

Chapter 51

The Housewife

*"The wise woman builds her house,
but the foolish tears it down with her own hands"*

Psalms 14:1 (NASB)

I had been a housewife for twelve years. I was completely devoted to being a good wife and mother. But now that my kids were ten and twelve, I was able to focus on my dream again. Many signs made me realize it was time to get back in the ring.

I was ready to fight for my dreams. Now I had to find the right photographer. The last pictures that were taken of me at the age of thirty-six, had opened many doors. The modeling world would say that I was way past my prime, but I had not even gotten married or had kids yet. I still felt young and attractive. And those anointed pictures opened many doors and even sent me to New York City to compete for the "Face of Avon." At that moment, I realized the power of a picture.

Where would I find the right photographer? My sister Wendy had recently gotten her pictures taken with a New York Photographer. His name was Barry Morgenstein. The headshot he took of my sister was a money shot. In the fashion world, it means a million-dollar picture. I needed a money shot to help jump start my modeling career at the age of fifty-three.

My sister gave me his phone number to call him. I was very intimidated because I had been a stay-at-home mom and had been out of the fashion world for many years. As I called him, I was shaking but knew I had to take a step of faith because I believed this was my destiny. I thought back to the two crowns I had won and realized I needed to reclaim my throne.

When Barry answered the phone, he was super friendly, and I felt a connection. I told him I was a stay-at-home mom and about my dreams to be a model. I am sure he heard this story a million times but not from a fifty-three-year-old woman! He made me believe it was possible, so we set a time and location.

When I showed up for the session, I was greeted by Barry. He was wearing a vintage tee with an American flag. He looked more like a rocker from the 80's and just like the song, "Born in the USA" by Bruce Springsteen, he was proud to be an American. This photographer took pictures of famous people including the news media, politicians, singers, actors, and models. Most people showed up in a conservative dress or suit. I showed up with a sexy dress and a bikini. I believe I was going through a midlife crisis.

When I received my pictures, my headshot was beautiful, but my bikini pictures had many flaws. I realized I needed a trainer. Lifting weights is the perfect workout to tighten and tone. I needed an expert to help prepare me for the next bikini shoot.

Looking back, it was one of the best moments of my fashion life. They had a hair and makeup team that was extraordinary. This team made me look like a supermodel and the photoshoot made my heartbeat again for my dreams. I knew this is where I belonged, and I was ready to risk rejection and heartache again to make it in the modeling world.

Many years later, I realized this was destiny and Barry Morgenstein was the first key player on the chess board. His passion and talent as a photographer would be the first move to help open the door, preparing me two years later to be the queen.

Chapter 52

It's Not Impossible

Then God Said, "Look! I have given you every seed-bearing plant throughout the earth and all the fruit trees for your food"

Genesis 1:29 (NLT)

During perimenopause and menopause your hormones spike. Most women claim they are unable to manage their weight. I noticed that I started gaining weight around my stomach. I started to look like I was pregnant every time I had a donut, pastry, or cookie. I will admit, I still eat my pumpkin bread! But I must think before I eat. I make my money as a beauty queen and model.

I had had a sponsored trainer during 2020 as Mrs. DC and was in the best shape of my life but now I was working out on my own again. I realized I was getting out of shape, so I hired Michelle Blake, her daughter was one of my Girl Scouts. Michelle was not just a trainer; she had her masters in exercise physiology. And her clients call her "The Body" after Elle Macpherson.

She was also an athlete that played division 1 soccer in college. She knew everything about eating right and working out. She is forty-eight and still has the figure of a twenty-five-year-old. I knew she was the right trainer. She made a meal plan for me, and now we meet twice a week for a strength training session. Her motto is: "When you shape your body, you also shape your mind."

At the age of fifty-seven, I have been selected to walk in Miami Swim Week. I believe it is possible to stay fit and healthy in your fifties and beyond. Do not let anyone tell you that you cannot be pretty or fit after a certain age. It is truly a mindset. Recently, I met a lady named Lourdes at Church that had fourteen children. She was in her fifties, beautiful and fit. We must have "NO Excuses."

You must decide to make the right choices in what you eat, portion control, weight training and cardio. Not everyone needs a trainer/nutritionist, but if you are serious about being healthy and fit, I believe this is the quickest way to the crown.

Chapter 53

Ray of Light

"Commit your way to the Lord; trust in him and he will do this;
He will make your righteous reward shine like the dawn,
your vindication like the noon day sun"

Psalms 37:5-6 (NIV)

Before being crowned Mrs. DC America 2020, I worked at a local pumpkin patch for six years in Ashburn, VA every October selling pumpkins. I also made my granny's poundcake, pumpkin bread, and pecan pie. I will share these recipes in the recipe section. I loved working at this pumpkin patch because I was a stay-at-home mom, and it gave me an opportunity to work for a local business and meet many people in the community. I was also able to bring my kids who would jump in the bounce houses for hours. My dog, Otto, with endless energy, would come with my husband at the end of my shift and race around the pumpkin patch. It was a joyful time for the whole family.

That is also how I met Tuya Sharav. This Mongolian beauty was tall, slender with dark hair and brown eyes. Her name means "ray of light." She came to the pumpkin patch with her daughter Joy. I was having a bad hair day and she told me she was a hairdresser. She was not just an ordinary hairdresser. Her mother was a hairdresser. It was in her family lineage. She had also trained in New York City and was an expert in color and styling. The best part was that she worked out of her van. She came to my house, which was so wonderful. I did not have to go to a salon. I felt like a celebrity.

As a future beauty queen, you need to have beautiful hair. I met Tuya in 2018. This is when I was also stuck in mom mode. She had an eye for current trends with hair, makeup, and fashion. I told her I wanted to pursue a modeling career. She believed in my youthful dreams and was going to do everything to help me get on the cover of magazines. She updated my hair and wardrobe. I was also wearing blue eyeshadow from the 80's just like Katy Perry in her video "Last Friday Night." She said I needed to walk into the 21st century. I had to change my eyeshadow color from neon blue to a neutral brown. This would highlight and not hide my brown eyes.

In 2019, at the age of fifty-four, I decided to rent a limo and asked Tuya and a group of my closest friends to go to the Watergate Hotel to celebrate my birthday. They have an amazing restaurant called Top of the Roof which overlooks Washington DC. I highly recommend this for anyone visiting the Nation's Capital.

Standing on the rooftop overlooking the heartbeat of the world, I was wearing my birthday crown. According to our society, being in your fifties is middle age and other cultures consider this old, but I still felt young. Maybe it was still possible to be a Queen. God saw that buried dream in my heart and he was getting ready to show me it wasn't too late.

One year later, I would be crowned Mrs. DC America 2020. Ephesians 3:20 states: "Now unto him that is able to do exceedingly abundantly above all that we ask or think, according to the power that worketh in us, unto him be glory in the church by Christ Jesus throughout all age, world without end." Tuya was a ray of light that helped guide me to the crown.

Chapter 54

No Media Requests

"But the natural man does not receive the things of the Spirit of God, for they are foolishness to him; nor can he know them, because they are spiritually discerned"

1 Corinthians 2:14 (NKJV)

One of my acquaintances in the fashion industry was being interviewed by a local station. Her full-time job is in the healthcare industry. She deserves to be interviewed for her incredible talent. I shared with her that I was upset I had never been approached to be interviewed by the network. I asked if she had contacted them. She said they had reached out to her. Then she said to me, "Why would they want to interview you?"

The moment I won Mrs. DC America 2020, I received hundreds of emails, texts, and calls from women congratulating me on winning this iconic crown that would lead me to the Mrs. America Stage. I believe I inspired women of all ages to see that at fifty-five it is not over; it is not too late, and you can still find your crown.

Through this book, I hope to continue to inspire many through my journey that your story has just begun. While reading a chapter to a close friend, she responded it will be a wonderful journal.

To me, everything I had gone through my entire life from feeling hopeless and unloved to winning the crown was more than just a journal. I had a story to tell about resilience and perseverance. I went through years of hopelessness and rejection. Then after being happily married for fifteen years and winning the crown, I became a public figure overnight, and helping others.

My platform for my reign led me to receiving a Presidential medal.

I believe this was worthy of a Royal Announcement!

Chapter 55

The Team

"Then the Lord God said, "it is not good that the man should be alone; I will make him a helper fit for him"

Genesis 2:18 (ESV)

Putting God first, accepting Jesus Christ, and following His ways is the most important decision you will make in this life.

The next most important decision you will make is choosing your husband or wife. You must be a team and build each other up and help each other achieve each other's dreams.

I love the iconic line in the romantic comedy *Jerry Maguire*. At the end of the movie, Tom Cruise said, "You Complete Me" to Renee Zellweger. That is how I feel about my husband. We complete each other and what I have realized after all these years is a team wins championships.

But first, I want to remind everyone reading this book that I went through endless failures. To change the story, you must realize nothing is ever hopeless and failure is not final. In my life, I have been deemed un-castable, overlooked, ignored, underestimated and even considered unlovable. The good news is there is hope. Are you going to accept the evaluation of what others think of you or are you going to evaluate yourself? God states, we are a masterpiece made in His image. You are the writer, producer, and actor of your own fairytale. Even though God is outside of time, on this earth, time waits for no one. Every minute counts.

Destiny is calling.

What is the assignment God has for you?

I decided to run for the crown of Mrs. DC after fifteen years of marriage. My husband was very shy, but he supported me by taking my hand and walking confidently out on the Mrs. America Stage to support my dreams. In that moment, on that prestigious stage, I realized it is never too late to find your crown.

Princess Pumpkin Bread

By JeanAnne Roberts

Ingredients:

2 ½ Cups White Sugar

1 Can Pumpkin Puree (fresh pumpkin or Libby's)

4 Eggs

1 Cup of Vegetable Oil

⅔ Cup Water

3 ½ Cups All Purpose Flour

1 tablespoon ground cinnamon

1 tablespoon ground nutmeg

2 teaspoons baking soda

1 teaspoon salt

½ cup miniature semisweet chocolate chips or raisins

Preheat oven: 350 temp. 2 (9 by 5) loaf Pans. Butter and flour pans. 1 hour bake time.

Combine sugar, pumpkin, eggs, oil, and water in a large bowl. Beat with electric mixer until smooth. Blend in flour, cinnamon, nutmeg, baking soda and salt.

Fold in chocolate chips or raisins.

Royal Poundcake

By Hazel Chafin

Ingredients:

2 Cups White Sugar

2 Cups Flour

2 Sticks Salted Butter (soft)

5 Eggs

1 teaspoon vanilla

1 teaspoon lemon

Mix for 10 minutes.

Preheat Oven: 300 temp. Bundt Pan. Butter and flour pan.

Bake for 1 hour.

ALMOST HEAVEN PECAN PIE

By Georgia Griffith

Pillsbury Pastry Pie Crust - Follow Directions on box.

3 eggs

⅔ cup sugar

½ teaspoon salt

⅓ cup butter, melted

1 can of corn syrup

1 cup pecan halves

Beat eggs, sugar, salt, butter, and syrup with mixer. Stir in pecans.

Pour into pastry lined pie plate

Heat Oven 350

Bake 40 to 50 minutes

To my audience:

It's not too late.

Go find your crown!!